Texas Boys in Gray

by

Evault Boswell

Republic of Texas Press

Republic of Texas Press is an imprint of Wordware Publishing, Inc.
No part of this book may be reproduced in any form or by
any means without permission in writing from
Wordware Publishing, Inc.

Printed in the United States of America

ISBN 1-55622-777-9
10 9 8 7 6 5 4 3 2 1
2003

All inquiries for volume purchases of this book should be addressed to Wordware
Publishing, Inc., at 2320 Los Rios Boulevard, Plano, Texas 75074. Telephone
inquiries may be made by calling:

(972) 423-0090

Contents

This book is a
condensed version of
Reminiscences of the Boys In Gray, 1861-1865,
compiled in 1912 by
Miss Mamie Yeary of McGregor, Texas.

Foreword

(From the 1912 edition by Miss Mamie Yeary)

In offering to the public these "Confederate Reminiscences" my only apology is to place in permanent form, and in the very words of the participants, as far as practicable, the personal experiences of the "men behind the guns," the "boys in the line," who by their courage, fortitude and patriotism, carved high up in the temple of fame, the names of our commanders and made them illustrious in the annals of war.

No claim is made to literary merit nor elegance of diction; neither do I give further proof of the correctness of the statements made than that they are recollections of the men who were in the "thickest of the fray"—men whose inspiration was fidelity to principle.

No one can rehearse the stirring events of the sixties as can the veterans themselves, and generations to come will bless them for giving these brief details of what they saw, did and suffered during those four years of carnage in defense of their homes and their rights.

Many interesting papers, too lengthy for the scope of this work, have been abridged to contain the most important parts. The reader will bear in mind that where a battle line was several miles in length that no one man could see it all, and that the different descriptions, seemingly at variance when taken together, make up the whole battle.

While editing the data so kindly sent me, I have entered fully into each skirmish, battle, march, and campaign. I have listened to the first shot fired on old Fort Sumpter [*sic*] in

Charleston Harbor at 4:30 a.m., on April 12th, 1861, and have followed you to the last engagement at Palmetto Ranch, Texas May 13th, 1865. I have been with you with Bragg in the Kentucky campaign; fought with you at Perryville and Richmond; mourned with you over the loss of the gallant Zollicoffer; came back with you through the snows at Cumberland Gap; stood with you in the battle line at Murfreesboro and Chickamauga.

Again I went with you with Morgan on his raid through Kentucky, through Indiana and on into Ohio, where he and a remnant of his daring followers at last surrendered.

I have been with you with "Old Pap" Price when you took your lives in your hands and went into Missouri; suffered with you from cold and hunger on your long retreat, and wept with you when you have left many of your comrades in the enemy's country.

Again, I was with you with Johnston in that masterly one hundred days' campaign from Dalton to Atlanta; marched with you with Hood into Tennessee and stood by you in the bloody battles of Franklin and Nashville.

I have witnessed Sherman's march of devastation from Atlanta to the sea; watched his wanton destruction of the defenseless homes in the path of his vandals.

I have been with you on your long and weary march into New Mexico, and returned with you to Texas to again take up the march into Louisiana, when you so completely routed Gen. Banks; saw your heroism at the bloody battlefields of Mansfield, Pleasant Hill, and Yellow Bayou, and have often wondered how men could live, exposed to the freezing winters and scorching summers, with no more protection than the beasts of the field.

After the battle of Elkhorn, I have gone with you to Shiloh and Corinth; then to the ditches of Vicksburg, where you dined on mule beef and pea flour, salted with hunger and a determination to win. I have gone with you with Stonewall Jackson through the Shenandoah Valley and mourned with you when that Christian military genius "passed over the river" at Chancellorsville.

I have been with you with Gen. Lee at Manassas and around Richmond; went with you into Maryland, fought with you at Gettysburg, saw Pickett's charge on Cemetery Ridge at Little Round Top; was with you at the bloody angle at Spotsylvania; witnessed the "blow-up" at Petersburg and went with you to Appomattox, where you stacked arms, furled forever the spotless banner of the South and then went with you to your desolate homes where you started life over again.

But life's battle is almost over with most of you. The last roll will soon be called and you will "pass over the river" to be with Jackson and Lee and Johnston, and all that long list of heroes with whom you fought and suffered through all those long years, and when "all is over" you may rest in the full assurance that a loyal people will still hold in grateful remembrance your heroic devotion to the principles which make men free.

If I shall succeed, in any degree, in preserving to the generations to come, a record of some of the deeds of daring, some of the privations, some of the sacrifices and sufferings of "that thin gray line" of immortals, who for four long years, held at bay the mightiest army of modern times, in an effort to give life and perpetuity to "a nation born in blood; a storm-cradled Nation that fell," I shall feel amply renumerated for my efforts.

My grateful acknowledgments are due especially to Gen. W. L. Cabell of Dallas, Texas; Mr. and Mrs. S. A. Cavit of McGregor, Texas; Miss Daisie Hale of Farmersville, Texas;

my uncle, W. P. Bickley, Farmersville, Texas; my mother, Mrs. J. K. P. Yeary, McGregor, Texas; Col. Milton Park, Dallas, Texas; and Col. W. L. Danley of Nashville, Tenn., besides the host of veterans, S.C.V.s and U.D.C.s for valuable assistance in the compilation of these Reminiscences.

Mamie Yeary, McGregor, Texas
Nov. 1st, 1912 Pearl Witt Chapter 569, U.D.C.

Preface

Texas was the largest state in area to enter the Union, although there was at one time a movement to split it up into four separate states. On January 18, 1861, at San Antonio, Brig. Gen. David E. Twiggs, commander of the Union Department of Texas, surrendered all Federal posts and property to state authorities before resigning his Federal commission and joining the Confederate cause. On the last day of his administration, President Tyler had announced that Texas had accepted and was a part of the Union. Its withdrawal from that Union did not come easily. None less than patriarch and legend Sam Houston opposed secession to join the Confederacy, but to no avail. If the Civil War created a "nation divided," it also produced a state that was rent asunder.

From all over the frontier state, thousands answered the call to arms, although most of them probably had no real concept of what the war was about. Texas blood ran from Gettysburg to Petersburg, from Shiloh to Iuka, from Vicksburg to Chancellorsville, and even to a multitude of minor skirmishes unrecorded in the history books.

And after forty-five years had passed, Miss Mamie Yeary of McGregor, Texas, decided the memoirs of these valiant Texans needed to be preserved and, through the Daughters of the Confederacy, conducted a survey of the surviving veterans in 1910.

Many of the veterans who lived in Texas at that time had not marched from the Lone Star State to fight, but had come to the land of escape and opportunity after the war.

"GTT" became a common sign hung on hundreds of doors across the South. "Gone to Texas" was a way to elude many of the deprivations faced by the local wars continued in most of the South and particularly in the border states such as Missouri, Kentucky, and Tennessee.

Some of the writers for Miss Yeary's book had even been to old Mexico with General Price and Joe Shelby, refusing to surrender and take "the oath."

But after forty-five years, most of the old wounds, both physical and mental, had healed and the old boys recalled as best they could their experiences. J. C. Blake of Longview wrote: My age is 72 years and time has caused me to forget much.

Time had taken its toll, and memories had either faded or been enhanced over the years of many tellings. Some wrote lengthy essays on their daring exploits while others only listed their rank and outfit.

However, a common thread winds through all the testimonies: It was a terrible time when men did terrible things to other men. The glory of war was lost in the suffering of the wounded and the confinement of the prison. It was a time when men with empty bellies performed extraordinary deeds in unbelievable fashion.

The Texas veterans of the Army of the Confederacy reported the war as they remembered it, both the good and the bad, the fear and the joy, the love and the hate. It is well to remember that in some cases these memories have been dulled, or enhanced, by the passing of time.

This compilation of these brief memoirs of these revered warriors will hopefully give us all a look inside the times and the amazing men who fought and died for a cause they could barely understand.

No effort has been made to correct the language or spelling of the memoirs, and colloquialisms are left as they were found in the edition of 1912. Obvious typographical errors have been corrected. Some punctuation marks have been corrected for clarification. The reader should be aware that the memoirs have not been changed, but recorded as the men wrote them. Some dates, places, and names may not be accurate as far as history is concerned. Footnotes have been added to properly identify the sites of battles and the names of commanding officers, or where other clarification was deemed necessary.

The comments on each memoir are the editor's and are only meant to be the substance that ties the stories of these remarkable men together.

At last when the guns had been silenced and the weary soldiers set their faces toward home, the Rebel spirit had not been stilled. The Rebel yell, though muffled by 1912, could still send fear into the hearts of enemies.

It will probably continue to echo through the ages.

References for the footnotes are: *The Civil War Dictionary* by Mark M. Boater, published in 1959 by Van Rees Press of New York; *The Civil War Day by Day, An Almanac* by E. B. Long, published in 1971 by Doubleday of Garden City, New York; and *Historical Times Illustrated Encyclopedia of the Civil War*, edited by Patricia L. Faust, published in 1986 by Harper and Row Publishers of New York.

Special recognition is due Michael Toon of the Texas Collection at Baylor University, and to Kathy Self and Patty Jenkins for their computer expertise.

Close Encounters

No other conflict in the history of the United States resulted in so much close hand-to-hand, or bayonet-to-bayonet fighting as did the war between the states. This is reflected in the memoirs of **Thomas J. Abbot of Aspermont**, a private in Company E, 17th Arkansas Regiment, General Little's Brigade, General Price's Division of the Army of Trans-Mississippi:

I took an active part in the hotly contested battle of Iuka.[1] *In this battle the armies confronted each other. Rosecrans*[2] *sent a brigade to the rear of Price's*[3] *army and then the battle began, which lasted three hours, during which we averaged more than forty rounds of ammunition to the man. When the battle began, the armies were about 400 yards apart, but after an hour of hard fighting, we advanced on the enemy to within about seventy yards. After another hour's fighting we advanced again to within fifty yards. We moved on double quick towards the enemy and when within the lines they fired one piece of artillery at us with canister shot; but we pushed on across their line. We captured nine pieces of artillery of "ten horse" battery, a sergeant and a private. As we were pushing on to the enemy's line the smoke was so thick that we could scarcely tell the enemy from our own men. This private who had been wounded cried out, "You are firing at*

---

1   Iuka, Mississippi, September 19, 1862.

2   Federal General William Starke Rosecrans.

3   Confederate General Sterling "Pap" Price.

your own men." I passed the word back and the order came to cease firing.

I asked the private to what company he belonged and found out he was with the enemy battery. I then passed this word back, and as soon as the mistake was discovered, the firing opened again. We pushed on so near the enemy that the last shot which was fired, the blaze of our guns met.

Oscar W. Alexander of Wellington, a sergeant in Terry's Texas Rangers, had not only a close call, but a lonely one:

I was under General Forrest[4] in this battle in East Tennessee near Morris Station.[5] We were ordered to dismount and cross the railroad near a stockade, where one hundred Yankees were hiding. We went on and crossed a fence into a field, came to a ravine when a call came for four or five to step out as skirmishers. I, with four others, advanced and went on in front of the stockade. About this time the command was ordered to fall back. We five went on, not hearing the command to fall back, and when we got near the stockade, Sam K. Tutwiler was shot through the left side, through the belt, but it proved not to be serious. Then Wm. Thornton was shot through the left thigh, missing the bone. W. E. Drisdale was shot through the right thigh, missing the bone. I turned to the right to see Drisdale, and found that he was the only one with me. I then went back to the command. But how the bullets cut the weeds and grass around and between my feet! Running on the grass like scared mice, I came out unhurt.

Dr. H. S. Arnold of Copperas Cove, in letters to his cousin, Miss Julia V. Nixon of Hinds County, Mississippi, wrote of a

---

4   General Nathan Bedford Forrest.

5   A skirmish took place at Morris Ford, Tennessee, on July 2, 1863.

narrow escape at the battle of the crater on the outskirts of Petersburg[6] on August 6, 1864:

Shells screaming and exploding overhead, one of which passed within two paces of the writer. Then came the big blow-up of the mine under the battery and the rush of Yankees to occupy the breach and especially the division of negroes,[7] and the slaughter in the "pit" of the crater. The carnage was so great that the Confederates stood in blood to their shoe tops.

S. O. Adams of Floydada was discharged because he was too young, but afterwards enlisted with the Tennessee Calvary:

I was not wounded, but was struck several times. Had bullet holes in my hat and in my clothes, but was never disabled.

P. J. Bailey of Farmersville served in the Missouri State Guards:

At the battle of Jenkins Ferry[8] were dismounted and sent forward to bring on the fight. We were in an old field where the mud and water was nearly knee deep. We were halted and ordered to lie down under fire, but there was no good place to lie down, so I kind of crouched down, when my Captain yelled out, "Lay down!" I said, "Lay down yourself," as he was standing upright. In this fight, every horse in the artillery was killed in about one minute.

---

6   Petersburg, Virginia, July 30, 1864. Miners from Pennsylvania dug a tunnel 586 feet long under Confederate positions and placed 8,000 pounds of powder.

7   Some reports state that Grant substituted white troops for General Ferrero's division of black troops the day before the attack with the division led by Brig. Gen. James H. Ledlie, who had drawn the short straw.

8   Jenkins Ferry, Arkansas, April 30, 1864.

Richard Johnson Barbour of Normangee, whose military career began with a literal bang, saw his first action at Fishing Creek, Kentucky:

My first experience of the horrors of war was at Fishing Creek,[9] Ky., an incident here impressed me deeply. We had a fine soldier in our company who said that if he had to be shot in battle, he wanted to be killed dead, and he was shot almost in the center of the forehead. I was so close to him his blood besplattered me, so I have never forgotten Travis McKinney.

Elijah Barr of Gatesville, after the battle of Galveston,[10] did not regret being in only one fight and was thankful he had no close calls:

I am not sorry that I was not in other battles, for if I had been I might have lost my life.

J. D. Boring of Merkel, as did many of the Confederates, served with two of his brothers and lost one at the battle of Gettysburg:[11]

R. M. Boring [brother] at Seven Pines[12] had both cheeks cut with minie balls, the tip of his thumb shot off, and his gun cut by a piece of shell. R. M. was killed at Gettysburg in Pickett's charge. He fell with the colors of the Fourth Georgia. He was not the color bearer, but picked them up when the color bearer fell. I think he was the seventh man that met the same fate that day.

G. E. Barringer of Farmersville had two horses shot from under him in one day and went home to get another, but his closest brush with death was behind a tree stump:

---

9   Fishing Creek, Kentucky, January 19, 1862.

10   Galveston, Texas, January 1, 1863.

11   Gettysburg, Pennsylvania, July 1-3, 1863.

12   Seven Pines (Fair Oaks), Virginia, May 31, June 1, 1862.

4

General Lane's[13] *brother and I were lying behind a small black jack stump and Lane asked me to move over a little as the shells were all coming on his side. I moved about four inches and just then a grape shot struck him between the shoulders and went entirely through his body. The shock threw him about ten feet, and when I went to him he said, "You can do me no good" and was dead.*

W. M. Belew of Blue Ridge was saved from a serious "gut shot" that would have most certainly proved fatal:

Was struck on the belt buckle at the battle of Murfreesboro,[14] *Tennessee. I was knocked down and the breath was knocked out of me and my comrades supposed I was shot through, but thanks to my belt buckle, I was soon all right.*

W. R. Bell of Blossom got very little thanks for saving his brother's life:

There was a pine tree in the way of one of the guns and my brother picked up an axe and started to cut it down. I pulled him back when just then a cannon ball cut it down. I said to him, "Where would you have been if I had not pulled you back?" "I don't care if it had," said he.

Newton A. Carter of Gainesville was with Wheeler's[15] army all the way from Atlanta to Savannah and in continual mix-up with Sherman's[16] calvary:

---

13 Probably James Henry Lane, affectionately called "Little General" by his men.

14 Battle of Stone's River, Tennessee, December 31, 1862 through January 2, 1863.

15 "Fightin" Joe Joseph Wheeler.

16 Federal General William Tecumseh Sherman.

Sometime we would strike them away from the infantry and would drive them to where they could be protected, but at Wayneboro[17] *they had a brigade of infantry to back them. We dismounted and formed in an open corn field. We had them in check for a while, but both the right and left wings of our line fell back and left the center, and the enemy closed in on us and surrounded us. Just at that time reinforcements came and we were relieved. Those who had me in charge were on horseback and were shot and fell either dead or wounded and when they saw they could not keep me one of them struck me an overhead blow with his saber, intending to split my head open, but I dodged and caught the blow on my neck and fell unconscious. As soon as I came to my senses I saw a heavy line of the enemy about 100 yards on one side and our forces about the same distance on the other, which left me between the contending parties. As soon as I was able to get up I made a run for our lines. The bullets from both sides, in the meantime, were cutting down the cornstalks around me, but strange to say, I was not touched by a ball. I have always thought that it was through the goodness and mercy of God that I ever got out of that place alive.*

M. A. Cooper of Breckenridge, whose brigade was commanded by General Bee[18] at the first battle of Manassas,[19] recalled that it was Bee who gave Jackson the nickname "Stonewall."[20] But Cooper had other things to worry about:

---

17 Waynesborough, Georgia.

18 Barnard Elliott Bee died in a cabin near Bull Run battlefield July 22, 1861.

19 Bull Run, Virginia, July 21, 1861. Manassas to the Confederates.

20 Some say Bee bitterly remarked that while his and Barrow's brigades were being annihilated, Jackson "stood like a stone wall," with his own brigade and failed to support the hard-pressed units. Others report it was a call to rally behind the Virginians.

At the battle of the Wilderness[21] *I received thirty seven holes through my blanket which was around my shoulders, one through my hat, and five through my canteen.*

James Marion Copeland of Atlanta also needed to repair his tattered wardrobe:

The next day we had a fierce engagement at Pleasant Hill,[22] *where we lost one Lieutenant and five or six men. I came out of the two days' engagement with nine minie ball holes in my hat and clothing.*

Even generals were not immune to close calls, according to the testimony of **Burton Rieves Conerly of Marshall**:

Gen. Lee[23] *rode along about fifty yards in front, between us and the battery on the hill, moving to our right. Just as he was passing a point directly in front of the Sixteenth Mississippi, a cannon ball passed under his horse, just missing his stirrups, and striking the ground bounded over us, missing the writer's head only about ten feet, afterwards striking the ground and disappeared. I was exchanging shoes with Archie Robertson at the time for the benefit of my blistered feet. Gen. Lee did not seem to lose his composure, but continued on his way to the right of our brigade, where he met General Harris.*[24]

In a few minutes, Archie Robertson was shot and fell dead in front of Conerly.

Miles A. Dillard of Blossom had a really close shave:

---

21 Battle of the Wilderness, Virginia, May 5 through 7, 1864.

22 Pleasant Hill, Louisiana, April 9, 1864.

23 General Robert E. Lee.

24 Nathaniel Harrison Harris.

Was not wounded during the war, but at the Battle of Murfreesboro[25] *had my horse killed and a ball passed through my whiskers.*

B. F. Frymier of Waco also had a brush with death:

We engaged in a fight at La Fourche Crossing,[26] *with 200 men against 800 of the enemy, who were behind breastworks and after a fight of about two hours, the enemy received reinforcements and we were overpowered.... In this fight, three comrades and myself advanced near the breast-works through a ditch in a sugar-cane field and when we were ordered to retreat I left three of my comrades on the field dead. I appeared to have a charmed life, for I was not even wounded, but a minie ball clipped out a bunch of my whiskers.*

Robert Augustus Brantley of Summerville served with Hood's Texas Brigade and made what could have been a fatal mistake at the battle of Manassas:

Reached Gen. Jackson the second day at Manassas.[27] *It was so dark we did not know each other. I marched out with a Federal and did not discover my mistake until I reached their campfire, then I turned for home.*

Solomon Thomas Blessing of Fort Worth and a Federal soldier both had reason to be glad for the inadequate equipment of both armies:

In the flank movements of Grant's "On to Richmond" campaign, after the battle we were in self-constructed breastworks dug with our bayonets. We were charged upon and

---

25 Murfreesboro, Tennessee, December 31, 1862 to January 2, 1863.

26 La Fourche Crossing, Louisiana, June 20, 1863.

27 First Battle of Manassas, Virginia, July 21, 1861, second battle, August 29-30, 1862.

some of our men were killed by bayonet thrusts, I received a bayonet wound in the hand. I had fired and reloaded and was capping my gun when a Federal mounted the works and aimed directly at me, but his gun failed to fire. I succeeded in capping my gun and aimed at him and mine failed to fire. By this time he had picked up a big rock and hurled it at me. Just then two Yanks came at me with fixed bayonets. I dropped my gun and by God's favor, got hold of both their bayonets and called, I surrender.

Like so many others, **J. W. Hodge of Ennis** had his clothes riddled with balls, but may have had a hard time explaining why the holes were all through the back of his shirt:

Received a saber wound at Jonesboro[28] on the head, but it was not a serious one. I was never taken prisoner. I broke and ran. They shot at me but only struck my shirt with thirteen holes and one struck the horn of my saddle.

It would seem that **John W. Higgins of Grapevine** would have learned to hide behind bigger trees:

In the battle of Dewry's Bluff[29] four of us were behind a small tree, ten inches in diameter and all were wounded except myself. In the battle of Ocean Pond[30] I had the bark knocked off of a tree into both my eyes. I shifted position and lay down behind an old stump, when a ball came through and stuck me in the breast, but had spent its force and did not hurt me.

Hopefully, **Samuel Gibson of Austin** may have been exaggerating when he reported:

---

28 Jonesborough, Georgia, August 31 and September 1, 1864.

29 Drewry's Bluff (Fort Darling), Virginia, May 15, 1862 and May 16, 1864.

30 Ocean Pond, Florida, February 20, 1864.

I was never wounded but had my clothes almost shot off me at different times. I don't know how I escaped.

C. W. (Victor) Reinhardt of Terrell wished his clothes had been hit, for he may very well be the most wounded man in the war, and the "etc." at the end of his list of wounds makes you wonder if there were others:

Was wounded in the head at Shiloh; in the ankle at Murfreesboro; in the eye at Missionary Ridge; in the belt buckle at Chickamauga; in the knee at Resaca; in the right leg at Atlanta; in the left arm by sword at Franklin; head and shoulders with gun butt; pinched with bayonet, etc....... I never missed a march, skirmish, battle or any other movement my regiment was in. Was never in the hospital, except the field hospital for emergency operation or treatment.

At a Confederate reunion in Houston after the war, **Pleasant K. Goree of Madisonville** and his comrade in arms Buck Carlton, who was called "Old Pap," had a laugh over a close encounter that was not so funny at the time:

One incident about an old comrade named Buck Carlton; During the siege of Petersburg[31] we had to take dispatches into the trenches every day. It came his time to go in. Several hundred yards of the way had to made by crawling, as one moment's exposure might have meant death. So, after he had been in, curiosity prompted him to stand up and look at the enemy's breastworks. While in this position some Yankee spied him and sent a shrapnel shell, which burst a few feet in front of him, and one of its contents made a round hole in his ear. He came out very much elated. Said he, "I have got a

---

31   The siege of Petersburg, Virginia, lasted from June 15, 1864 to April 3, 1865.

furlough. Look at this hole in my ear." But the doctor told him he could fight about as well as ever, and he got no furlough. At the Confederate reunion at Houston I was getting a shine when someone put his hand over my eyes from behind and asked me to guess who it was. After failing, he asked me if I remembered Buck Carlton, and I told him that if that was Buck Carlton he was marked in the ear, and sure enough, there was the hole.

Tyre Hancock of Dallas marched almost continually for a year before he got in the battle of Carrion Crow Bayou[32] and then wished he had missed it:

We were formed in line of battle in a valley and were told that the enemy was just over the hill. We raised the "Rebel Yell" and charged. I saw a fine large tree on top of the hill, and was determined to get to that tree, which I did, and fired the first gun direct at the enemy in the valley below. I was not scared until I looked back and saw that I was far ahead of my command. Greene Duncan was mortally wounded just as he passed my tree, and Nathan Walker and I picked up poor Greene and took him off the field under the heaviest fire of shot and shell that I ever experienced. We laid him behind a log and started back. Just then I saw Tom Greene's Cavalry charging the enemy's rear. At the same time I looked and the enemy's cavalry was charging our rear. There was some hard hand to hand fighting, and many were killed and wounded. Five or six of their cavalry ran through our line and were coming straight at us firing with their pistols. Nathan was a good runner and got away. I fell like I was killed and escaped.

---

32 Carrion Crow Bayou, Louisiana, skirmishes October 14, 18 and
     November 3, 11, 18, 1863.

Johnson Busbee Harris of Karnes City had a brother John who was eighteen when the war started, and his younger brother Henry was fifteen. Henry was sixteen when he had his brush with death:

My brother, Henry Harris, 16 years old at that time, was home on a furlough. Some Yankees came to the house. When they saw him one Yankee raised his gun and took aim. My sister, Bettie, saw the movement. Henry was ten feet away from the muzzle of the gun. It meant certain death. She rushed and knocked up the gun. He missed his aim. In the surprise and confusion Henry escaped.

J. H. Harrison of Ranger, who fought with General Bragg[33] in Kentucky, found that even in the heat of battle, it is wise to check your gun:

In a charge at Richmond, Ky.,[34] we routed the enemy. I saw four or five men run behind a haystack and asked a comrade on my left if he saw them and he said that he did, and that we would get them. We were running and at the same time loading our guns, stopping and shooting. On reaching the hay stack my comrade went around to the left and I to the right. I had discharged my gun just before reaching the stack and had reloaded but had failed to put a cap on. A Yankee ran around on me, and as I was not able to shoot, I caught the muzzle of my gun let drive at him. He dodged and the gun struck the ground and broke off at the breech. When I struck at him and seeing my gun broken, I seized his with both hands. He could not shoot me but we had it around and around until the other boys came up and captured him. He was a man that would weigh 180 pounds while I was a mere boy of eighteen years.

---

33   General Braxton Bragg.

34   Richmond, Kentucky, August 29 and 30, 1862 and July 28, 1863.

Sam A. Griffith of Paris had his brush with death at the battle of Corinth:[35]

On the evening of the second day's fight at Corinth, Oct. 5th and 6th, our command was the second line of battle, and we had to crawl through brush and cut timber for hundreds of yards, under the galling fire from the enemy. Within thirty yards of the entrenchments, I had not fired a gun and had forty rounds of ammunition around me and could see about one dozen men shooting at us. They were firing through the port holes where a battery had been. Finding a friendly post oak stump about eighteen inches high, I used it for my breastworks while I shot at the Yanks through the port holes, taking deliberate aim at one man at a time, until they all disappeared and I had discharged my last cartridge. I ran up the works and had arrived near the top, when the Yanks reinforced and rose up from one end of the works to the other, those in front of me being not more than ten feet away. When I looked behind me to see where our men were and could see none but dead and wounded (they had retreated) I decided to run out, and luckily I struck a wagon road that wound around through the debris and kept in it. The enemy did not fire on me until I had gotten 100 yards from the works. Then they opened fire on me all along the line and kept it up until I reached the timber. You would have thought it was general engagement, if you had heard the firing. I was the last Confederate to leave the works near Old Battery Robinett,[36] which was the closest place I was ever in.

Edward Freeman Comegys of Gainesville said that he was never badly wounded, but he sure came close a few times:

---

35 Corinth, Mississippi, October 3 and 4, 1862.

36 Located at Corinth, Mississippi. Battle of Corinth took place on October 4, 1862.

Had my hat shot off at Chickamauga[37] and my canteen punctured by a ball. My right ear was slightly cut at Petersburg, and my boot heel was shot off at Drewry's Bluff.[38]

B. L. Vance of Como decided perhaps it was his clothes the Yanks were mad about:

I was struck by a spent ball and knocked off my horse and stunned for a short time. They tried to shoot the clothes off me; one time they split my hat open.

And **Bennett Wood of Temple** learned to even dodge the missiles:

Solid shot were falling near us, and glancing up in the direction from which they came, I saw a ricochet shot coming towards me. I fell forward saving myself, but Smiley fell by my side, his entire head shot off.

Losing a hat would have been a welcome relief for **W. F. Renshaw of Quinlan**:

It would be impossible to tell of the suffering from hunger and exposure at Vicksburg. We had to stay in the ditches and take the rain as it came, as we had no shelter, and then the heat and cold with shot and shell, and hunger. When Gen. Grant made one of his desperate charges on our breastworks a bayonet in the hand of one of his men tore the skin off the top of my head.

J. R. Jones of Carrigan talked himself out of a close encounter:

I was wounded at the battle of Jenkin's Ferry,[39] being shot through the hip. When I came to myself there was no one on the battlefield except myself and the dead and wounded. In a

---

37 Chickamauga, Georgia, September 19 and 20, 1863.

38 Drewry's Bluff, Virginia. Battles on May 15, 1862 and May 16, 1864.

39 Jenkins Ferry, Arkansas, April 30, 1864.

short time after I became rational the Yankees sent a line of skirmishers on the battlefield. They were all negroes except the officer. One of the negroes threw his gun on me to shoot, but I begged him out of it.

John D. Shipp of Farmersville couldn't talk his way out of a tight spot, but he could shoot his way out. Being captured by bushwhackers was not the best thing that could happen to Rebel or Yank:

I was one of Hill's scouts in Northern Alabama, and was captured by what were known as Tories under Flowers (they did not belong to the regular army). I supposed they would kill me, but they had a negro cook with them, and they thought he was a great shot, and they said I might shoot it out with him. I told them that if they would give me my pistol and let me load it I would try him a crack. They agreed to this and stepped off the ground, and we turned our backs together and at the command wheeled and fired. I felt his bullet close to my head. He was hit between the nose and the mouth. They gave me my pistols and let me go my way.

W. H. Jones of Brady not only survived his close call, but saved his lieutenant:

The last evening at Missionary Ridge[40] when the brigade on our left gave way, Cheatham[41] on their right and my regiment on the right of the Division. Two other comrades and myself heard no commands and saw no movements and were left. The Lieutenant ran back to tell us that we were left and we started. Lieut. Jones was wounded, and he asked me not to leave him, so I took him astraddle of my back, but by this time, the Yankees were so close they were trying to halt me,

40 Missionary Ridge, Tennessee, November 25, 1863.

41 General Benjamin Franklin Cheatham.

but I carried him out, out running them and their bullets, carrying him four miles to Chickamauga Station, and put him on the train. If living, he can be found at Waverly, Tenn. I give this reference because it sounds "Fishy." He weighed about 145 pounds and I 185. I thought afterward that I could have caught a quart of bullets in a pint cup if the bottom had held.

William Howard of Brownfield tells of a comrade who had a narrow escape:

New Hope Church[42] May 25 to June 4, was a hotly contested battleground. I am told that the timber on the battlefield died from the effects of shot and shell. The lines of battle were entrenched within 80 to 100 yards of each other. I remember one day we got up a conversation with each other as the firing on the line ceased. One of our men, Bob Goodlett, proposed to meet one of their men on halfway ground and swap newspapers. So it was agreed. Goodlet jumped over the breastworks and started. The Federal got on the breastwork on his side and said: "Go back, Johnny Reb; they wont let me." Goodlet got back just in time, as the bullets soon came thick and fast.

Just bending over saved the life of **P. E. Korff of Cost**:

Was in the siege of Vicksburg. In the trenches at Vicksburg.[43] My second Captain, B. I. Sterling, and Lieutenant were both down sick with fever, suffering for want of water, and I volunteered to bring them some from a well about a mile off. Both objected to it as the bullets flew very thick. Coming back by a place where soldiers had camped, I

---

42   New Hope Church, Georgia, May 25 to June 4, 1864.

43   Vicksburg, Mississippi, from October 16 to December 1862, and April 1 to July 4, 1863.

saw a piece of canvass and stopped to pick it up. A cannon ball struck a tree, and if I had been standing there a moment longer it would have cut my head off. I succeeded in getting the water.

J. W. Jackson of Crowell survived by what must have been a miracle:

Was wounded at the battle of Knoxville,[44] Tenn., shot in the right shoulder; toe shot off at Chancellorville,[45] and hit on the head with a bombshell at Fredericksburg.[46]

After suffering his third wound of the war, **Theophilus Franklin Meece of Livingston** could hardly catch his breath:

Was severely wounded at Second Manassas. Was severely wounded in the right arm and slightly in the left groin at Gettysburg, Pa. on July 2, and at second White Oak[47] was shot in the neck, the ball lodging against the upper posterior portion of the shoulder blade, cutting my windpipe and swallow. I breathed through the wound until closed by lint.

F. H. C. Perry of Seymour was a lot luckier:

Was struck by a spent ball in the forehead at Franklin, Tenn.

A close encounter at the battle of Seven Pines involved the entire Fifth Texas regiment, according to **Wm. Henry Mathews of Livingston**:

Very late in the afternoon on the day of the battle, our regiment (the Fifth Texas), from some means got separated

---

44 Knoxville, Tennessee, campaign of November and December, 1863.

45 Chancellorsville, Virginia, May 2-3, 1863.

46 Fredericksburg, Virginia, December 13, 1862.

47 White Oak Road, Virginia, March 31, 1865.

from the remainder of the brigade and while we were lost it became very dark and rainy. It was so dark that we could not see twenty yards, not knowing where we were nor where the enemy was. Our Colonel gave orders for us to lie down right where we were, although we were wet and cold, we went to sleep, at least I did. Just as it was getting light enough to see well, we discovered a Yankee camp about two hundred yards from us, some of them were up cooking breakfast and quite a number had not gotten up. Our guns were all loaded and we raised the rebel yell and charged them. They broke and ran leaving everything they had, a few took their guns, but nothing else. We captured their breakfast, cooking on the fire, and a great variety of commissaries.

Z. McDonald of Commerce found that a soldier was never safe, even at leisure:

While the two armies were skirmishing we were laying around waiting for the battle to come on. I was lying with my head on a comrade's leg for a pillow, when the Federal skirmishers spied us and trained a small piece artillery on us. The first shot struck the ground at McCoy's head and exploded and I thought had blown his head off but only powder-burned him. Scared? I should say so. I could hardly stay there.

Next to prison and hospitals, the men feared being captured by bushwhackers, who were apt to kill you whether you were a Yank or a Reb. **Isaac Perry of Speegleville** got lucky:

At Williamsburg, Ky., I was captured by the bushwhackers and taken off to be shot (at least that is what they said they were going to do with me), but after robbing me of all my money and knife and clothes, they turned me loose, but told me that I would not go half a mile till I would be shot.

F. M. Smith of Waco was saved, and almost killed, by a piece of his equipment:

The Fourth Alabama was 650 strong and was soon in line and double-quicked to Bull Run and put into position near the Henry House where we fought one hour and fifteen minutes, firing by command. We had smooth bore guns and when I had fired my ninth round a minie ball struck my cartridge box and set my ammunition and clothing on fire. I have the minie ball now which was found in the box.

Francis Freeman Scott of Blooming Grove had more than bullets to dodge:

In my first battle, my comrade next to me, Foster, fell across my lap with a bullet in his head and dying while Collins fell on the other side saying, "Scott, I am shot." I told him to be still and soon the poor fellow knew no more. The enemy was picking them off so close to me that I got up and moved nearer to them, getting behind a big oak tree. No sooner had I done so than a cannon ball cut the top off and I ran from under to keep it from falling on me and to my surprise I found that my whole regiment was gone. How I ran to overtake my comrades and was glad to catch up with them.

Henry Pool of Lindale was lucky to survive a head shot:

At Alltoona Mountain I was shot between the eyes and they were about to leave me but I determined to get in the ambulance. I was carried down the mountain and I guess I fainted for I paid no attention to them putting those in the ambulance who were only slightly wounded. I raced up and told the doctor that I was going too and he said there was not room for any one else, but I told him if he did not let me go I would never fire another gun. They thought I would die, but I got up and ran to the ambulance and got in and got away.

Like many others who fought in the western sector, **R. R. Williams of Cumby** was caught on that thin line that separated regular soldiers from bushwhackers:

Was made prisoner on Jan. 24, 1864, carried to Fort Smith and was sentenced by court martial to be shot for guerilla fighting. I was forced to dig my own grave, but got a new trial and proved by Federal soldiers that I was a Confederate officer and was released from the sentence of death and afterward made my escape.

Henry W. Strong of Paris escaped capture by taking to the sea:

My brother had a company gathering cattle for the army, and they were in squads under an officer who gave vouchers on the government for the cattle. My brother had sent me to Mobile for money to pay the vouchers, and on my return trip when I reached the ferry on the Baloxi Bay the old negro ferryman told me that I had better help him all I could as there was a ferry boat up the bay which seemed to be watching the ferry. When we were nearly across and working for dear life, the old negro said; "Now I tole you so. Jes' put your eye on dat over yonder," and on looking toward the Gulf I saw a gunboat turning the point about a mile and a half away. "Pull, honey; maybe dey won't see us."

My money was in an old haversack, and I tide a bolt to it so that I could sink it in the water if I had to be taken. The old negro kept working. We were some distance from the shore when to our surprise a shot was fired in front of us, and up went the old negro's hands, and he said; "Honey, jump you horse ofen the boat an' you can make it. The water ain't mor'n saddle skirt deep, an' it may save you from goin' to Ship Island." I did so, and they began shelling the woods, and kept it up for an hour or more.

William R. Waller of Seymour decided that he was a member of the "Army of Texas" and fought the war on the Texas coast. One of his adventures is lengthy, but worth the telling:

In was the desire of the commander of the Confederate forces to learn the strength and position of the Federals on Matagorda Bay. I volunteered to secure this information. I was ordered to report at headquarters with a man to go with me on the scout. After considerable delay I found Thomas B. Carroll, a sixteen-year-old boy, a private of Company C, Thirty-Fifth Texas Cavalry, who volunteered to go with me. Armed and mounted we left our camp on the 6th of January, 1864 at 9 o'clock at night. we proceeded down the bay, passing our guards, and just before daylight passed our last scout. It was so foggy we could not see ten paces. When the wind rose and lifted the fog, to our dismay we saw that we were cut off by a large party of Federals, whom we had passed unobserved on account of the fog. We were ordered to halt and surrender, but we darted down the beach at full speed. The gunboats turned lose their shells, grape and canister on us. The bursting of shells and the whistling of grape and canister made it lively for us until we passed the Federal fort in easy gunshot. Near sundown we discovered a vessel at the lower end of the peninsula disembarking troops. In a short time the Federals were advancing from above and below and were closing in on us.

Closer, closer, they came. In this trying moment the sun slid down behind the western waves. This was the pivot on which our liberty turned. Darkness hovered around us while we hid ourselves in the waters of the bay. The enemy came and went, but found us not. As the Federals retraced their steps, we followed and viewed the surroundings. We counted the vessels. They numbered nine sails. Some of them were large men-of-war. We even saw the watchmen in the rigging.

After satisfying ourselves, we tried to get out of their lines. So close were the guards that it was impossible to pass. We then concluded to bury ourselves in the sand and drift and remain until the next night. So we dug a hole and spread a blanket over it, and Carroll and I laid down in it. I covered the traces possible with sea weeds, and there we remained until the next night. We could hear the regular tramp of the sentinels, the rattling of the officer's swords and even understand what they were talking about. At 9 o'clock on the night following we crawled out and again attempted to get through the lines. We determined to cross an arm of the bay nearly half a mile across. So into the water we went, carrying our ammunition and our guns above our heads. A part of the time the salt water came up to our chins, but finally we reached land. We traveled all night and reached our camp in an exhausted condition.

John Q. Thompson of Troy went to war with an unusual weapon but managed to avoid death or capture:

My first weapon of war was a spear with handle on it about eight feet long; my next was an old-fashioned bored hunting rifle, for which I had to make or run my own bullets and make my cartridges. My next was an Enfield rifle, which was won on the battlefield.

At the battle of Jenkin's Ferry, that gun failed him:

Will Chambers, a boy of 18 years, and one of the color guards, caught the flag before it fell to the ground and waved it in the lead and shouted, "Come on boys." After the charge was made, orders were given to fall back and fire on the retreat. I failed to hear the order. Five of us took shelter behind a large oak tree. All were shot down except myself; my gun became choked. I threw it down and picked up one of my comrade's guns, who had just fallen by my side, and kept up firing as if I was not alone until I discovered the enemy charging on me. I took deliberate aim at a group of the enemy, fired and then retreated in double quick time.

J. J. Amason of McGregor, at the battle of Shiloh,[48] believed in following doctor's orders, up to a point:

We formed the right wing of Sydney Johnston's[49] line. The Fifty-Second Tennessee was fighting the Federals in their tents and Johnston ordered the old Ninth Arkansas to help them, and into it we went. We were ordered to our knees. Some obeyed and some did not. I for one was soon put out of business. My arm was broken and I went to the rear to have it dressed, and lo, and behold, it seemed that my whole regiment had been wounded. The doctor dressed my arm and told me to bathe it in the branch to stop the blood, which I did till a bombshell fell in the water by me, and I left.

J. W. Boyd of Hawley probably headed for a clothing store when he got home from the war:

I was a sharpshooter at the time Petersburg[50] was blown up. I counted twenty-seven holes in my clothes which had been shot there during the night.

The Federals also wreaked havoc with the wardrobe of **John Simpson Daughtie of Nacogdoches:**

Was slightly wounded in the left arm in July, 1864, and had my clothes torn by bullets and my hat shot off several times.

---

48 Shiloh (Pittsburg Landing), Tennessee, April 6-7, 1862.

49 Albert Sidney Johnston of Kentucky was killed in the vicinity of the Peach Orchard.

50 Battle of the Crater, July 30, 1864.

At Fort Donelson, **Alfred Hicks Douglas of Prattville, Alabama**, found that he could not even enjoy a good meal when the opportunity presented itself:

On Wednesday everything was very quiet in front of us. I remarked to the Captain that it would be a good time to send back to the fort for something to eat. He ordered me to take seven men and go over for provisions. We sent a negro cook ahead of us, and on our arrival he had all provisions ready. After we had been eating a few minutes the gunboats attacked our land batteries. About the third shell ricocheted and came through our cabin, passing just over our heads, tore down our stick chimney and cut out three logs.

M. F. Holbrook of Longview was only fifteen years old when he was put on picket duty:

Once while on picket one and a half miles from camp, with two other pickets between me and the camp, I was ordered to shoot. Just at daylight two Federal soldiers rode within about 100 yards of my post and stopped. According to orders I fired on them and they returned the fire. The two pickets between me and camp fires to give the alarm. I thought the enemy had got between me and the camp was trying to kill me. Just imagine how lonesome a fifteen-year-old boy would feel with death staring him in the face from both sides.

At Pleasant Hill, **John Howard King of Gilmer** found there was danger not just from the sides, but from above, too:

At Pleasant Hill[51] so many horses were killed that the citizens piled them and burned them. For miles along the road there were wagons deserted where the Federals had but loosed their horse and left. Here was the wildest shooting

---

51 Pleasant Hill, Louisiana, April 9, 1864.

that I saw during the war. They shot the tops off the trees all to pieces, and we were more in danger from falling timber than from bullets or cannon balls.

At the Sugar House fight, King found himself in danger from wood again:

The Federals were in a three-story sugar house, with the fence (a rail fence) about two hundred yards away, was laid down, every other panel, and our men were in the corners of the fence. Here my face was showered full of splinters, but not a bullet hit me.

John H. Lewis of Mabank was glad to find cover in a canebrake after a ditch and log had proved to be unsafe hiding places at the battle of Milliken's Run:[52]

We came to a ditch with some brush along it and hid ourselves. Pretty soon the Yankees came on us with 300 skirmishers, and their commander said: "Boys, when you get there, just make the hair fly." Capt. Bonner told us to hold our fire till he gave us orders, and when they were within about twenty or thirty yards of us he gave the order to fire. Jeff Robnet shot the commander off his horse. John Wallace and I picked out two men just in front of us, and when we fired they both fell. Then our regiment reinforced us, and the Yankees fled. Some prisoners told us we killed forty. We had two wounded. We stayed at the ditch, the sharpshooters firing on us, but we could not see them. I laid down behind some elders about three feet high, and I suppose they saw me lay down, and began shooting at me. The first shot cut the elders on one side and the next cut a swath on the other side, so I got away. But they threw bombshells at us, and we had to lie

---

52   Milliken's Bend, Louisiana. A number of events took place here, but no major battle.

close to the ground. Soon about 500 cavalry charged us. It was about fifty yards to a canebrake, and I ran for dear life, and they shot at me at every jump. I got on a big cypress log and looked back and they were in about twenty steps of me and shooting at me. So I made for the canebrake and was soon out of sight. After much running and fighting I got away. You have heard of the "small dog in high rye." Well, it was nothing to a man in a canebrake trying to fight Yankees and get away at the same time.

L. N. Perkins of Plainview was only in the battle of the Wilderness for short time, but it proved to be an exciting time:

Before going into battle, a cousin, Emory Perkins, and I agreed that if either of us were wounded the other would carry him off the field. My wound in the head naturally dazed me and I ran backward through my company. "Em" saw me and ran with me until we came to a branch, where he bathed my wound until I became conscious. Our regimental surgeon rode up about that time and cut the bullet out of the back of my neck with his pocket knife.

A head wound, like a gut wound, more often than not spelled death, and the medical personnel usually chose to help those who they felt had a chance of living first.

But **J. B. Sutton of McGregor** reported on a close call of his brother-in-law, Dick Hardcastle:

In 1864 my brother-in-law, and three cousins of mine were brutally shot by the Yankees, who had been told that these boys were stealing horses and keeping them on an island in the Tennessee River. This was not true. They had their own horses there to keep them away from the Yankees, but they got a pilot and the boys were arrested and marched off to the river bank to be shot. After examining the pulse to see that all were dead they were rolled into the river, but Mr.

Hardcastle was shot in the shoulder and, of course, no pulse was noticeable, and when he was rolled off into the river he strangled and several shots were fired at him; but he caught a limb and was quiet till they left, when he scrambled out and went to a skiff and was soon at his sister's, where he was treated and is still alive.

David H. Williams of McGregor was also glad to be alive after playing dead, almost literally in the mouth of the cannon:

Then the next was at Winchester,[53] *but Early had cleaned them up pretty well so we had nothing more to do till we got to Gettysburg on the 2nd of July, 1863, and went into battle on the 3rd. We charged the first line at the barn on the left of the peach orchard and carried the place with very small loss. We then passed on to the second line and charged a battery where we had a heavy loss and I was shot down in twenty feet of the cannon, and was reported dead and lay there till midnight, but the boys captured the battery and turned the Federal's guns on them.*

Anthony A. Bryant of Frost was wounded several times, but escaped serious injury in spite of a hailstorm of bullets:

Was first wounded at the battle of Sharpsburg, Md.,[54] *a flesh wound in the left thigh. Was also wounded at the battle Gettysburg, Pa., July 1, 1863, in the right foot; at Petersburg, Va., I was shot in the arm. Was never in prison. I was one of the old "Blue Hen's Chickens." I have been shot at and told to halt when bullets were falling like hail around me, but I heard them not.*

---

53   Winchester, Virginia. Two battles were fought here: May 25, 1862 and June 14-15, 1863.

54   Sharpsburg (Antietam), Maryland, September 17, 1862.

Bullets were not the only danger faced by **C. C. Eoff of Carlton**:

Was in guerilla warfare in Arkansas, and was shot twice in the arm after I had surrendered. I had eleven holes shot in my clothing. Six were killed, six wounded and six captured. I was taken prisoner in the above battle, but escaped with the enemy shooting at me; jumped off a bluff twenty-five feet high.

William F. Glaze of Athens had a close call at the battle of Peachtree Creek:[55]

The Peachtree Creek battle was another short but fierce fight. It was on the 20th of July, 1864. Here I was shocked by a shell exploding close to my head. It did me no harm except to make me deaf for awhile, and my head roared all next day.

---

55 Peachtree Creek, Georgia (Hood's first sortie), July 20, 1864.

The Halt, the Lame, and the Dead

In a war where amputation was one of the primary medical procedures and a wounded man might lay in the field of battle for days, death was almost a preference. Field hospitals were little more than butcher shops, and the makeshift hospitals in homes and churches were a good place to die. But the indomitable Rebel spirit, the love of life, or perhaps the fear of death helped many men overcome some of the most horrible wounds inflicted on man by his fellow man.

J. H. Harrison of Ranger solved his minie ball problem in a very peculiar way:

A ball entered behind my ear, ranging downward and lodging in my wind pipe. I coughed it up.

Perhaps the most embarrassing close encounter occurred to **A. T. Ball of Valley View,** who enlisted in May 1861 at Windsor, Missouri, in the Windsor Guards, Trans-Mississippi Department:

I was wounded by my own gun at the battle of Cole Camp.[1]

Matthew Deloach of Cumby found hospitals not to be a haven for rest from the perils of the fighting:

At the siege of Vicksburg[2] *my foot was shot off by the explosion of a shell on the first day of June, 1863. I was*

---

1   Cole Camp, Missouri skirmish on October 6, 1864.

2   Vicksburg, Mississippi, second campaign, July 4-10, 1863.

captured at the surrender of Vicksburg on July 4, 1863..... This was an every day fight until I was wounded. Then the hospital was bombarded.

C. B. Deishler of Mason received his "red badge of courage" at Harper's Ferry:[3]

Here, after three quarters of an hour the enemy charged us. I looked around to see how many there were and found that we had been ordered to fall back. Ben Hubbard and two others and I were all that were there. We saw the regiment going up the mountain about two hundred yards from us. The bullets were falling fast behind them and the smoke so dense we could scarcely see our men. I suggested to the boys that we go down the rock fence into the woods and join the Third Alabama. After our arrival there, I jumped the fence and learned that the enemy's line was about forty yards from us. The other boys got behind the fence and I ran. They shot holes through my haversack and clothing. I had run about one hundred and fifty yards when a bullet struck me in the wrist. I dropped my gun and caught up my arm. My three comrades were captured, but I got up the mountain out of the range of the enemy's guns.

Mason went to the field hospital where he found four of his comrades wounded and rejected some advice:

The surgeons examined my arm and told me to go to division hospital, as I would have to have my arm amputated. I thanked them and told them that I was not likely to find it. They informed me as to where it was and I told them not to put themselves to any trouble directing me.

---

3   Harper's Ferry, West Virginia, October 13, 1864.

Apparently Mason and his arm survived, for he was with Lee at Appomatox Court House and dictated his memoirs to his granddaughter, Jennie Gipson.

John E. Logsdon of Gainesville was another sufferer who did not want to find the hospital:

We took an active part in the battle of Chickamauga.[4] Then we were with Johnston's army in the summer of 1864. During this protracted campaign my health became very poor. Some of my comrades tried to get me to report on sick list and be sent to the hospital. I told them no, not as long as I could walk. I would rather risk my chances on the firing line than in any army hospital.

It is difficult to comprehend the suffering of the wounded, such as **W. J. Dean of Marquez**:

Was shot through the body at Seven Pines,[5] May 1862; also received a slight wound in the leg at Sharpsburg and at Chancellorsville[6] was shot through the head and lay on the battlefield five days and nights. One of my comrades stayed with me.

Indeed, we have to wonder how so many survived such terrible wounds, considering the medical attention available. At the battle of the Wilderness, **J. W. Deane of Blum** was wounded:

Was wounded at the Wilderness,[7] the ball striking me on the cheek bone and coming out the back of the neck.

And at Sharpsburg, **Q. D. McCormack of Goldthwaite** saw perhaps the ultimate wound:

---

4   Chickamauga, Georgia, September 19-20, 1863.
5   Seven Pines (Fair Oaks), Virginia, May 31-June 1, 1862.
6   Chancellorsville, Virginia, May 1-4, 1863.
7   Battle of the Wilderness, Virginia, May 5-7, 1864.

I was also in the battle of Sharpsburg,[8] *where many men were killed on both sides. One of my comrades had the misfortune to lose both arms and both legs in this battle.*

You would probably not expect his fellow soldiers to call **William Lott Davidson of Richmond** "lucky." Davidson enlisted at San Antonio on August 1, 1861, and served in Company A, Fifth Texas Volunteers:

At the battle of Val Verde[9] *on the 21st of July 1863, I had the end of my little finger on my left hand shot off. At Glorietta*[10] *was shot through the left thigh. At Galveston, Jan. 1, 1863, was shot through the left arm. Had a saber cut in head at Cherryville, Kansas. At Brazier City [1863] was shot through the body and was shot in the thigh at Yellow Bayou*[11] *in May, 1864.*

But perhaps Davidson was fortunate when you consider the death of his comrade in arms:

Jim Whittenberg, killed at the capture of the Granite and Wave in 1864. Had his right hand shot off and begged not to be taken to the rear, and then when both his legs were broken he still begged to be allowed to remain; still he fought until a cannon ball cut off his head.

Louis H. Becker of Terrell found that even in camp, there was no guarantee of safety:

My only wound was from the accidental discharge of a pistol in the hands of Louis Daughtery of my company.

---

8   Sharpsburg (Antietam), Maryland, September 17, 1862.

9   Valverde, New Mexico Territory, February 21, 1862.

10   Battle of Glorieta Pass, New Mexico Territory, March 26-28, 1862.

11   Yellow Bayou, Louisiana, May 18, 1864.

D. A. Edwards of Celeste was not only wounded seriously, but taken to prison where medical care was at a minimum and stayed for over two months after the war was over:

I was wounded in the battle of Winchester,[12] *Va., on Sept. 19, 1864, the ball entering the corner of my mouth and breaking my jaw bone. I was captured at the same time and sent to Point Lookout,*[13] *Md. Was released from prison on June 27, 1865.*

D. F. Fields of Frost helped a man who had a most unusual injury:

Was east of Atlanta on the Decatur road when one of our men had the front part of his skull shot off, but it did not break the membrane around the brain. Another comrade and I carried him to the rear and laid him behind a big stump while the other went for an ambulance. I had to hold his hands to keep him from tearing out his brains. It was a sickening sight. I would like to know if he got well, and if the comrade who helped me is still alive.

Even nature sometimes took its toll, as reported by **Elias Fikes of Waco**:

We were then transferred to Mobile, Alabama, crossed the bay to Tensaw Station where we encountered a severe storm and had two men killed by lightning.

W. R. Bell of Blossom, as were so many others, was astounded by the dead at Franklin:

I helped bury the dead at Franklin,[14] *and I think I could have walked all over the battlefield on dead men.*

---

12   Winchester, Virginia, second battle, September 19, 1864.

13   Point Lookout, Maryland, the largest prison in the North, established in August 1863.

14   Franklin, Tennessee, November 30, 1864.

B. F. Carpenter of Gainesville looked back over the years and counted the cost:

Our regiment went out of Texas with 1180 men and when we surrendered at Canton, Mississippi, there were 240 at roll call.

William J. Chandler of Farmersville did not survive the war, but his friend Tom Howard gave a report on him:

Bill Chandler was not a talker, but when he was called on or when volunteers were called for, he stepped to the front without a word and was ready for duty. He was the only man killed at Cabin Creek.[15] He was wounded in the bowels and we put him on a litter and started to carry him off the field. We had gone but a short distance when he said he was dying and was soon gone. We dug his grave with our big knives, and as his blanket was bloody, I wrapped him in my own. He was buried where he fell. Such was the fate of many a good man.

Whether buried where they fell, or in a mass grave, many a good man was placed in the Southern soil. In winter the frozen ground made burial difficult, and in hot weather it became a necessity that the dead be laid away as soon as possible. **John L. Odom of Sulphur Springs** was on a burial detail at Chickamauga:[16]

We were held in reserve until Sunday evening about 4 o'clock, when we were ordered into service and fought until dark. We were under Gen. Longstreet in this fight. Had my knapsack shot off. That night the Federals left. The next morning our regiment was among those detailed to bury the dead. After getting our own men buried, we buried the

---

15   Cabin Creek, Indian Territory, September 19, 1864.

16   Chickamauga, Georgia, September 20, 1863.

enemy. We would dig a pit 6 x 8 feet and 4 feet deep; fill the ditch about three-fourths full of the dead, and then cover them with dirt.

Luther Wellington Murray of San Saba spent a rainy night listening to the cries of the wounded:

On July 1, at or near sunset, we went into the fight at Malvern Hill,[17] which lasted until about midnight. Here we made charge after charge, and our loss was heavy. We were ordered to take a battery in front, but we did not succeed, as there were six guns and well supported by infantry. It was now midnight, and the rain was pouring down, and four of us lay on the field until day, unable to sleep on account of the cries from the wounded, who were calling for their people, water and assistance in every way. As soon as we could see, we began carrying the wounded to the field hospital, to be cared for.

In a war with such terrible weapons of destruction, finding all the parts to bury could even be a problem, as **Milton Par of Dallas** remembered after seeing his friends killed:

In the battle of Resaca,[18] Ga., four of my comrades, John Rushton, John McLeod, Ed. Reeves, and Jno. Ozier, were killed by a single shot from a battery which enfiladed our lines on that fateful Sunday morning. They were all from Pike County, Ala. In the battle of Harrisburg,[19] Ky. Corporal Isaac N. Jones of my company, was killed by a fragment of shell severing his head from his body.

---

17   Malvern Hill (Crew's Farm), Virginia, July 1, 1862.

18   Resaca, Georgia, May 14-15, 1864.

19   Probably Harrisburg, Mississippi.

But the bane of **E. L. Morris of Reisel** was neither bullet wound, shell fragments, nor even death, which at times might have been considered welcome:

I had bad health; had pneumonia twice, measles settled in my lungs; had typus fever, mumps, and contracted catarrh from which I am still suffering.

Even the death of an enemy was traumatic, especially when you got to know him, as **T. C. Mitchell of Fort Worth** did on the battlefield at Murfreesboro:[20]

While on picket that night I had for company a wounded Lieutenant from an Ohio regiment. I was fortunate in having a full canteen of water from which he drank, but after doing all I could for him, when the day had ended he had closed his eyes in death.

Wm. M. Pennington of Breckenridge gives an indication of the suffering that took place on the long marches from one battle to another:

Next was the battle of Missionary Ridge.[21] This was a hard fought battle, and the bombardment was fearful. In the afternoon our line was broken, and we were forced to fall back to Dalton, Ga., barefooted. I feel the effects of this march today. Some had been frost-bitten and were sent to the hospital at Altanta, Ga. One soldier's feet sloughed off at the ankles on account of being frost-bitten. Many lost their toes.

And Pennington witnessed a strange accident on the march to Dalton:

We had to break the ice on the march to Dalton, Ga., and swim a small stream . One poor fellow built a fire to dry his

---

20 Murfreeboro (Stone's Mountain), Tennessee, December 31, 1862 to January 2, 1863.

21 Missionary Ridge, Tennessee, November 25, 1863.

clothing, and laying his gun down near, the leaves burning out to where the gun was, it shot and killed him instantly.

L. N. Perkins of Plainview gives a vivid and horrible account of his injury and an insight as to why many preferred risking death rather than reporting to a hospital. It was here he learned that surgeons always took care of the injured who they felt had a chance to survive, while those who they thought had little or no chance were left until last:

We were now in Gordon's Division, Terry's Brigade. About 3 o'clock p.m. our ammunition having been exhausted, two comrades and I went back to the ordinance train for more. Sheridan's cavalry were flanking Breckenridge's Division on the extreme left of our line of battle, and to help them out we three boys fell in line with the Forty-Fifth Virginia Regiment. In a few minutes a piece of artillery took position in front of us at a distance of 800 to 1,000 yards. I was watching this piece and knowing that we were in an exposed position I suggested to my comrades that we move to the left. I saw the smoke from the gun, and that was the last that I saw of the battle of Winchester.[22] When the shell exploded it took off my right leg, a piece striking me about midway the thigh, knocking the bone out for about four inches and leaving a hole that I could easily run my hand through. With the help of two other men, my two comrades put me on a blanket and carried me to a big brick house on the battlefield, shook hands with me and left me, believing my wound mortal. They barely escaped being captured with me. This house was soon filled with our wounded, and was used as a hospital for four days. Our wounded who were not able to get off the battlefield themselves were all captured, and our own surgeons were left or sent back to care for us. I lay on the bare floor for

---

22 Winchester, Virginia. A number of skirmishes took place here.

four days without any attention except water being poured on my wound a few times. After all the other wounded were cared for, the amputations performed and the patients sent to the hospital in the city, the surgeon took off my leg and sent me to the hospital, where I was put on the first floor with nothing under me but a blanket. On the fourth day after this I felt that something was wrong with the wound and called to the nurse to come and see what was the matter. He raised the blanket which covered me and a stream of blood flew almost to the ceiling. Together we screamed for help, and the surgeon came and caught up the artery which had broken loose, but not until I had lost almost all the blood I had left in my body. After this I was better cared for, which was largely due to the attention of the good ladies of the city. Among them was a Miss Russell, whose kindness to me I shall never forget. I improved rapidly until I was able to be sent to prison. I was released from prison at Point Lookout,[23] *Md., June 4, 1865, and sent to Richmond, Va., and from there I had to get to my home in Grayson County as best I could. I walked on my crutches about 100 miles, and reached home June 18, 1865.*

Making the decision to go to the field hospital was not an easy one, but **A. G. Anderson of Fairfield** was willing to crawl there if necessary:

As we charged very near the last breastworks there came an order to retreat in good order. I was shot down just in front of the breastworks. Soon I found myself trying to decide whether or not I was killed. I saw that I was not dead, but bleeding freely, and that I must get to the field hospital. I crawled as fast as I could, but began to get blind from the loss of blood. At the edge of some timber I found a pond of water and plunged into it. Soon I heard parties not far away and

---

23 Point Lookout, Maryland, the largest of the Federal prisons.

found it to be Gen. Smith, who had been wounded. He told his surgeon to put me on his horse and we soon came to a residence which was being used as a field hospital, and after the General had been attended to he told the surgeon to attend to Anderson. My arm was dressed and soon after all the wounded were sent to Jackson, Miss., except those they thought would die, and I, amongst others, was left at Griffin, Ga. A few days after my arrival I found that my old friend, G. A. Rackstraw, had written his brother-in-law, Mr. Crowden, to look after me, and he and his beautiful daughter came and brought me soap and towels, a bowl and pitcher, (things I had not seen for a long time) and many delicacies to eat.

Anderson recovered enough to ride a mule to Jackson, Mississippi, but his wound was not healing and the doctors decided he was dying by degrees from the diseased bone:

They removed the bone at the shoulder joint and cut the other off just above the elbow. I came out from under the chloroform before the operation was complete and saw them stitch up the wound from the shoulder blade to the elbow.

The sound of battle was deafening, and in the case of **W. H. Arnold of Robert Lee**, it was literally deafening at the battle of Mansfield:

My hearing was affected greatly during the war on account of being so near the cannon. I was with a company of 303 men, and when we went into a battle we were formed near the artillery in order to keep the enemy from getting the cannon. A cannon discharged so near me once that the drums of my ears were shattered so badly that the blood ran from them, and I have never been able to hear an ordinary conversation since.

But it was not only guns that killed and maimed, as **W. E. Boyd of Queen City** discovered at Vicksburg:

Our first camp near Vicksburg[24] was in a hollow near a branch and many of our men took sick from using the branch water and a number died; John Garner, my brother-in-law, among the number. Our company at one time was 128 strong and not more than twenty were able for duty and it was found that the "town boys" could stand the hardships better than those raised in the country.

William F. Glaze of Athens was wounded near Atlanta, Georgia, and it brought an early end to his military service:

Our next battle was near Atlanta, Ga., on the 22d of July, 1864. We went into the battle about 1 o'clock in the afternoon, after having marched all night. And up to that time we had neither slept nor eaten since the morning of the 21st, and had nothing in our haversacks, but had filled our canteens with water as we waded the creek. We all knew that Gen. John B. Hood of Texas was in command, and that fighting was the order of the day. But alas, for me! Soldiering was to be a thing of the past. We had just got into the fight and were warming up to the work when I was shot through both legs, which put an end to my military career. I spent the remainder of the war in the hospital and on furlough at home. I was quite a young man[25] then but was crippled for life. Still, I have worked and earned a living, and have never received a pension.

Pleasant K. Goree of Madisonville was only two years older than Glaze when he fought at the Wilderness:

---

24 Vicksburg, Mississippi. Several campaigns and a siege took place here in 1863.

25 Glaze was seventeen years old when he was wounded.

*One of the sad experiences at the battle of the Wilderness was; While riding over the battlefield in company with Gen. Fields,[26] where the dead and dying of both armies were so thickly strewn that we had to be careful where we rode, I heard someone calling my name, and I found it to be the Lieutenant of my company, **William Robinson, of San Jacinto, Tex**. He was mortally wounded, and begged most piteously to be taken out, which Gen. Fields was prompt to have done, as some litter bearers were near at hand. We held the ground of this battle for two or three days, and tried to bury all the dead we could. The first night I went to the ravine from which we had been drinking to fill my canteen with water, and found it well mixed with blood.*

At Fort Donelson, **John R. Graves of Colorado**, another mere boy who had joined the Confederate cause, also found bloodstains:

I left school when but a child of fifteen years and enlisted in the Confederate Army against my parents will. Our regiment was organized at Camden, Ark., and we marched to Gaines Landing, on the Mississippi River, there took a boat for Memphis, and were then rushed to Fort Henry. We were shelled out of that place, and rushed to Fort Donelson, on the Cumberland River. I lost my knapsack and blanket on the march, and when we arrived at the fort it began snowing and sleeting, and we built trenches. Arrived at the fort about the 8th or 9th of February, and fought some every day; but the main fight came off on the 15th. It was a bloody day; the snow was red with blood, and I was all this time without anything to eat or a blanket to sleep on.

---

26 General Charles William Fields.

W. E. Hare of Glendale told another painful and bloody story:

For many days we were destitute for food. My clothing consisted of one shirt and a pair of worn-out jeans trousers, which my mother wove for me before leaving home, and old palmetto hat made by myself. We were compelled to sleep in the open air, enduring the cold and the rains. While in this destitute condition my feet were frozen. Notwithstanding my bare, bleeding feet, I was compelled to do my regular duty. We marched to a place twenty-five miles east of Alexandria, where we received a ten day's furlough to go home and get clothing. On my homeward journey, one could have easily tracked me by the blood from my feet.

Frank Herron of Graham was filled with passion and excitement as he charged across a corn field at Raymond,[27] but it soon turned to terror and despair. Then he met an angel who brought the joy of living back:

Onward we went with the rebel yell, driving the enemy back through a corn field and across a deep narrow creek. Here we were ordered to lie down and continue the fight in this position. In the last charge which our regiment attempted to make I was wounded. When I was first struck I supposed I was killed and when I saw the blood running to the ground I was sure it was true. I did not seem to have any great fear of death but what worried me most was the thought of dying so far from home and loved ones. With the assistance of my gun I hobbled to a tree for shelter. Soon one of my comrades came to assist me from the battlefield, but he was seriously wounded before starting with me, so another, a messmate, came to help me and he, too, was wounded. Our command was repulsed and in a little while I was captured

---

27 Raymond, Mississippi, engagement on May 12, 1863.

and sent to the field hospital where my wound was tenderly dressed by a Federal surgeon. This hospital was at and around the home of Mr. McDonald, a Southern planter and noble gentleman. Mr. McDonald and his family were allowed one room of their house and the remainder was used by the Federal officers who were wounded. In a few days the wounded Federal officers were moved to the town of Raymond and the rooms were used by the wounded Confederates. My wound had not been dressed in six days and was giving me great pain.

I believed I was going to die. While there my attention was attracted to a beautiful girl standing in the door with tears trickling down her cheeks. Her true Southern heart was bleeding and she was overflowing with profound sympathy for us wounded men and boys. For a short time I was transformed into a new creature. My wounds ceased to pain me and I wiped away the tears which had moistened my cheeks. In a few moments this girl came and sat down by me and took my hand saying, "Have you a father and mother?" She then procured a basin and some water and washed my face and combed my hair, as best she could, and then brought me something to eat. After this she made an effort to cleanse the clotted blood from my wound and found to our surprise that the wound was full of worms.

Herron was transferred to the hospital in Raymond soon after that and received daily visits from the young lady, who he came to know as Myra McDonald and later became Myra Dennis of Jackson, Mississippi.

I will never forget the kindness and tender care of Mrs. Myra Dennis to a wounded soldier boy of fifteen, and if I can pay the debt in no other way, I will endeavor to pay it in gratitude.

Herron added a final note to his memoirs about his hospital stay that is interesting:

I wish to mention a command which I heard Gen. Grant give to the Chief Surgeon at the field hospital. It was this, "Give the wounded men every attention which it is possible and make no distinction between Federals and Confederates." This is not given from report. I was within twenty feet of him when he gave the order.

William Howard of Brownfield didn't like hospitals, even if his was a church, and got out as quickly as he could:

Our wounded were taken prisoners and we used a church as a hospital. I was given a berth in the pulpit. I was very weak from loss of blood, but did not stay there long, but made my escape the sixth night.

Howell S. Wallace of Coleman gives one of the most vivid descriptions of a field hospital:

I was wounded in the calf of the leg, and as Gen. Anderson passed along I told him I was wounded, and he told me to do the best I could for myself. I started to the rear, dragging one foot. I had to go across a wheat field and very slow at that. Part of the way was in range of the bullets, and I could hear them and see the wheat falling all around me. With much difficulty I got to Hood's Division Hospital. The doctors had taken charge of a large barn and converted it into a hospital. Late in the evening I went up to the hospital to see if I could find any of my comrades. The sight I saw was too horrible to relate, if I could. At the back door I saw what seemed to me to be a wagon load of arms, legs, and hands. I turned and walked back, and never went there any more.

James Jackson Suttle of Abilene was determined his leg would not end up in the wagon:

As well as I can remember, we fell back into the ditches about the first of May, and on the 23d I was wounded. I was then taken to the hospital, and was there till July 4, which was a long, long time for me to lay and let the water drip on my wound. The doctors thought my leg would have to be taken off, but I believe the water saved it, and I have used it for many long years since then and it has been a great blessing to me.

At the battle of Belmont, General Gideon Pillow[28] had his softer side exposed, as recorded by **H. B. Dollahite of Lytle**:

The Yankees said that we were firing lamp posts at them. The gun was leaded the third time, but was not fired until after the battle. During this time we landed, marched off the boat with Gen. Frank Cheatham[29] in the lead. He pulled off his hat and waved it a few times, calling upon the men that had been routed to fall in line, which they did. By this time the Yanks were in full retreat, and before we commenced the pursuit Gen. Pillow rode up with tears in his eyes. He had ordered the Fifteenth Tennessee Regiment to charge bayonets through an open field. They were mowed down like grain before a scythe.

---

28 General Gideon Johnson Pillow of Tennessee.
29 General Benjamin Franklin Cheatham of Tennessee.

Christ in the Camp

For most of the Rebels, the war had begun as a glorious adventure, friends waving and ladies serving cookies and tea along the parade route. But by 1864, war had become an empty bellied, ragged, shoeless hell, and many of the Confederates surrendered not to the Federals, but to the Gospel as one of the greatest revivals in the history of the nation broke out in the Southern army. But from the beginning, with leaders such as Thomas "Stonewall" Jackson, J. B. Gordon, and Robert E. Lee, the South was certain that God was on their side, and if not, he would certainly not aid the damn Yankees.

J. M. B. Field of Willis was sent off to war by his mother whose farewell to her son was:

Go my son, and be a valiant soldier for your country. God be with you, farewell.

Solomon Thomas Blessing of Fort Worth enlisted in the Confederate army at Galveston with all the protection he needed:

I received a neatly bound copy of the New Testament. Inscribed were the names of three young ladies of the Methodist Church. My pastor, T. W. Wesson, gave me a handsomely bound copy of the Bible. Both of which I carried all the way and brought home with me. The testament had a corner shot off at the battle of Darbytown Road.[1]

---

1   Darbytown, Virginia. Battles took place here on the 7th and 27th of October 1864.

Many of the soldiers found the battlefield and camp a fertile field for evangelism, such as **J. N. Chandler of Granbury,** a captain in Company A, Twenty-fourth Georgia Regiment:

While in the army, I preached whenever occasion offered. While in camp I built a small school. I sent 100 testaments and divided my 100 men into classes of twenty, and gave them two chapters in the testament for a lesson, recited once in the morning and once in the afternoon, prayers and singing before hearing the lesson. In a short time, I had a class of over three thousand soldiers and officers. I preached to them on Saturday night and Sundays.

R. M. Gano, pastor of the Christian Church in Dallas, reflected on his service to the Confederate cause and the ministry of Christ:

On all occasions I have tried to do my duty and should all my converts remain faithful when I reach heaven I will meet an army of soldiers for Christ.

John Overton Casler of Oklahoma City recalled the battle of Chancellorsville:[2]

Charlie Cross, Sam Nunnelly, Jake Fogle, and myself were together when the shelling started. Found a low place where a tree had blown down in the past and laid in it. Shells seemed to be missing us by six inches. Jake Fogle kept praying all the time. Every time a shell would pass directly over us, Jake would say, "Lord, save us this time." Sam Nunnelly, a wild reckless fellow would laugh at him and say, "Pray on, Jake, pray on." The two kept that up during the shelling. Cross and I tried to get them to shut up but it was useless.

G. W. Anderson of Austin was quick to give God credit for his safety:

---

2   Chancellorsville, Virginia. Battle took place from May 1-4, 1863.

I was buried by a shell once, and another burst within two feet of my head. Thank God I was saved and protected by Him.

After the war, like many Rebels, **Lacy Boone of Fort Worth** became a preacher:

I was licensed to preach the gospel in March of 1868, and I have tried to make as good a soldier for Christ as I did for my beloved Southland.

Jacob Hemphill of Haskell was a lad of seventeen when he entered the Confederate army as, in his own words "a very wicked young man" but was decorated for valor. But after a wound at Sharpsburg,[3] he went home on furlough for six months and married Miss Emily V. Jernigan on December 8, 1862. After the war, he returned to his family:

I returned to my old home in Walker County, where I had a wife and sweet little babe awaiting me. The sad recollections of the dreadful days of 1861 to 1865, and the horrible "reconstruction days" bring bitter tears, only solaced by the thought that through it all, I was loyal and true to the cause, never flinching where duty called, and best of all, my help-meet was a Christian, and through her life God pointed me to a better life.

We can only imagine the tears falling on the page as **M. F. Holbrook of Longview,** who enlisted in the Confederate army at Laredo, wrote his emotional and flowery memoirs:

I often think of the sickness and sights of the battlefield where hundreds of men and boys lay wounded and calling for parents, some for sisters, groaning and reaching out their hands for help that could not come. It was awful. We can only bow our head and say, "God, in His infinite wisdom and

---

3   Sharpsburg (Antietam), Maryland, September 17, 1862.

according to his own Divine purposes, touched their tired hearts with that wand of eternal silence and the trembling lights of brave hearts and noble young lives went out. Earth's glory had been taken to add to heaven's treasures. But what was all the desolation of war in comparison to our own beloved youths, who lay sweltering in their blood, with the tear stained cheeks of the loved ones at home looking for those to come who had gone to that bourne from above shores none ever return. But the aching frame and fevered brow had been kissed by the angel of rest and their throbbing hearts had been stilled, and it remains for us to bow in submission to the Giver of all good and say, Thy will be done.

S. C. Littlepage of Waco joined the army at Springfield, Texas, in the early part of the war. A Methodist preacher, he was stationed at LaGrange, Texas, where he reported one of the most glorious revivals he ever saw. But the next year he volunteered as a missionary to the army and joined Walker's Division soon after the fight at Jenkin's Ferry,[4] Arkansas:

I traveled with the army, visited hospitals, preached to the soldiers at night and on the Sabbath, ministered to the sick and served the boys in every way I could. I organized four army churches in our division. I overtaxed myself, and my health gave way, and the doctors told me if I ever expect to get home I had better start then. I took them at their word and left camp near Minden and rode ten miles the first day; the next I rode fifteen miles, and on Saturday evening reached New Salem in East Texas, where I found Rev. Neal Brown and a Baptist preacher holding a union meeting, and they insisted that I should preach next day at 11 o'clock. I did so, and, as it was the first congregation to which I had

---

4   Jenkin's Ferry, Arkansas engagement on April 30, 1864.

preached which included women and children, it was inspiring, and I was just sick enough to preach my best.

The next day, the Baptist preacher took up an offering of four hundred sixty dollars to assist in the army ministry. Littlepage went home and rested for six weeks, raised another five thousand dollars, and headed back to the army, supplying the soldiers with the gospel, along with stationery, tea, coffee, tobacco, and medicine. He was, however, not without his critics:

I heard of one man who denounced me for speculating on the soldiers, but the matter was taken up by another, who asked him how much he paid a quire for paper and was told $30. "The parson sells it to us at $10," he said, "and if the boys have no money he gives it to them just the same." Finally my money ran out and I visited Galveston, Houston, Chappell Hill, and Brenham and other places and received donations from generous people and distributed to the boys free.

John L. McCord of Brekenridge, who was only fifteen when he entered the service, was probably exposed to Protestant religion in the revival that broke out in the last year of the war and contributed to the establishment of the Bible Belt:

Had the measles so bad. Fought at Jackson,[5] Mo. and with Price on raid. I enlisted in the army of the Lord as a Missionary Baptist in 1870, as a preacher in 1877, and am still in the fight at the age of 63 years, and would be so glad to recommend to all my old comrades to surrender to this same Captain, if they have not yet done so. Live for Him, and meet me in Heaven.

---

5   Skirmish took place at Jackson, Missouri, on September 24, 1864.

Stonewall Jackson, perhaps more than any other Confederate leader, was the epitome of Christian faith and dedication to the Southern cause. Like Lee, he would stop and have prayers before a battle with the men. The love of God and the love of the Confederacy became almost one, as attested to by **J. B. Marshall of Henrietta**:

We were put in Stonewall Jackson's Army as soon as the Seven Days[6] fight around Richmond was over, and we followed him until he was killed at Chancellorsville. He had the confidence, love, and respect of every man in the army, and we never lost a battle in the Eastern Army as long as he lived. I have the hope of meeting him and many of my old comrades where we will have a grand reunion and part no more. God bless the dear old Confederates. I shall ever love and honor them. I joined two armies, when a boy—the army of the Lord on the 27th of May, 1857, and the Confederate Army on the 27th of April, 1861. I am proud of them both, and have tried to be a good soldier in both armies.

The Bible-bred believers who marched off to kill their enemies did not always forget the admonition to love your enemies, as Mrs. Sue McLemore of Winnsboro reported when writing the memoirs for **Luther A. Williams of Sulphur Springs**:

In a skirmish one day Luther Williams became separated from the boys in making his way back to his command. He passed an abandoned cabin, hearing groans, he thought perhaps one of his own men might be in the cabin, he looked in and saw a Federal officer was wounded. When the officer recognized him as a Confederate soldier, he begged him not to kill him. Williams told him he was after live Yanks, and to

---

6   Seven Days Campaign near Richmond, Virginia, June 25 through
     July 1, 1862.

have no fear; he placed the officer in a comfortable position and as it was a cold day he built a fire, left fuel handy, filled his canteen with water, placed his knapsack by his side, and left him to his fate.

The fervor with which the Southern preachers presented the gospel led to great revivals in the army, and like all good pastors, **Frank McMillian of Hillsboro**, a Methodist preacher, made sure the boys took their newfound religion home with them. McMillian was born in 1823, and his memoirs were apparently written by a relative, although he was still alive when the survey was taken:

Col. Joe Johnson raised a regiment in Limestone, Freestone, Bell, Hill, and other counties for service on the Texas coast, and Rev. McMillian re-enlisted in Capt. John Oliver's company. For two years he did military service on Galveston Island and along the Texas coast. During this period he and others conducted protracted meetings, and many confessed religion under his preaching. It was common to organize soldier churches, and if a soldier was discharged and went home he was given a letter which transferred his membership to his home church.

The writer of the memoirs added an interesting final note:

The war left Rev. McMillian much poorer, he having several negroes who were of great value.

Aug. Schilling of Houston told of the loss of a good friend:

One of my best friends and good comrade with whom I shared my blanket many times, was killed at Milliken's Bend.[7] We were going on a forced march and just at the break of day we encountered a large picket force which opened a

---

7   Milliken's Bend, Louisiana. Several skirmishes and engagements
took place here.

terrible fire on us. My friend and I were riding side by side and he was killed by the first volley. He pulled a small Bible out of his bosom and told me to send it to his mother in Washington County. This young man was a German. For several days he would read in his Bible and look downhearted. I asked him what was the matter and he said he felt that something was going to happen to him. He was a model Christian and amongst all the surroundings of camp life he kept his innocence. He was the only son of a pious mother. May he rest in peace.

And after four years of bloody fighting and even more years of reminiscing, **John S. Kritzer of Taylor,** a private in Company E of the 2nd Missouri Cavalry, confided in his memoirs:

I have the roll of my company. Most of them are dead and gone to Heaven, I know, for a Confederate soldier could not go anywhere else.

J. G. McGown of Marshall looked at it from a different angle, while profiting from the war as much as possible:

I made $6,000 out of Union men and bushwhackers. Took their horses and mules and sold them and kept the money. I have no apologies to make for the part I took. Under the same circumstances I would do it again. It is hard for me to believe that the Devil would have any use for a good Confederate soldier.

Most of the Confederates were from the vast farms and small towns of the South, their lives vested in their families and their church. Many had premonitions about impending death in battle that perhaps those ties that bind had never been entirely broken. **Miles A. Dilliard of Blossom** spoke of one such incident at the battle of Murfreesboro:[8]

After this battle was over I was told that two of the boys said that when we were forming the line that they would be killed that day, and some one remarked to them; "If I felt that way I would speak to the Colonel and not go into the battle." One of them replied that the boys might think he was a coward, and he had rather die than be called a coward. They were both killed that day.

Sam Griffith of Paris told of a young man who seemed to know he was going to die:

Second Lieutenant P. G. Mosley, of my company, was killed in the first day's fight at Corinth,[9] Oct. 5, 1862. He had a presentiment of it before going into battle, and said to me, "Sam, I am going into the fight, but will never come out alive."

At the battle of Jonesborough,[10] Georgia, **H. C. Latham of Dallas** had a friend who had the feeling:

My poor messmate, Criswell, gave me his Bible with wife's and children's hair in it and said; "I will be left on the battlefield." So he was.

And again at New Hope Church,[11] **William B. Lay of Prairie View** expressed a similar incident:

I wish to speak of a dear comrade and messmate, a noble boy, three months younger than the writer. At New Hope Church, Ga., he remarked that he was going to be killed that day. About four o'clock in the afternoon Johnston[12] ordered

---

8   Murfreesboro, Tennessee, December 31 to January 2, 1862 (also known as Stone's River).

9   Corinth, Mississippi, October 5, 1862.

10   Jonesborough, Georgia, August 31 to September 1, 1864.

11   New Hope Church, Georgia, May 25-27, 1864.

12   General Joseph E. Johnston.

the whole line to charge and we took three lines of breast-works. We lost 249 men, and among the killed was the boy of 17, John Wells, who said that he would be killed.

Albert F. Jones of Temple tells of a friend who had the feeling he would die in battle and that Jones might die also:

One of my comrades, Ballard Laws, was killed at Knoxville, shot through the head. Before we went into the battle he told me that he felt like we would not come out all right, and if he should be killed he wanted me to promise to write his father, and if he lived though and I did not, he would write for me. So next morning I wrote the sad intelligence to his father.

F. P. Gillespie, who reported his memoirs from **Los Angeles, California**, told of a dream he had that sounds much like a letter from John the Revelator:

During a spell of typhoid fever I had the following dream, which may not be wholly uninteresting. In my dream or vision during the wasting fever, which was devouring me, it seemed that a strange messenger took me by the hand and led me up on the side of a mountain, around the base of which ran a railroad. The messenger bade me "Look," and pointing to the North, said, "See!" and behold darkness enveloped me. I heard screams and groans and ravings, as if a mighty engine was passing over those who were wailing and grinding them to death under its ponderous wheels. I stood in a bewildering fright and astonishment, when this stranger touched me again and said: "This is the doom of the South." The awful noise and darkness passed by and a streak of light, such as often follows an angry cloud, appeared. The light came hurriedly on, increasing in brightness, and as it swept by me seemed more dazzling and brighter than the rays of the sun. Then the strange messenger touched me again and said; "The future of the South." I gazed on the scene as it passed on to the South and my sight seemed unbound. Waving fields of grain and boundless acres of snow-white cotton spread out before me. Cities, teeming with millions of men and women, railroads running in every direction, made a scene which no pen can picture, and yet I have lived to see it more than realized. What was revealed to me banished doubt from my mind. Yet the dream was realized far differently from what I expected or hoped it would be. A kind Father was directing the storm and has accomplished or fulfilled the dream, and today we stand in the glare of that bright light which swept before me on the brow of that mountain. Even the grand principle of "States Rights," for which we fought and for which so many brave men bled and died, still lives; and our enemies have been forced to admit that they are the correct principles of our government. These principles have been maintained at a terrible sacrifice, but it could not have been otherwise. God knew best and the freedom of the negro established the freedom of white men on still firmer basis and the South will eventually be the "home of the free" as it has always been the "home of the brave."

The Terrible Cost and Hardships

There is no way to measure the amount of suffering experienced by the Confederate soldier, especially as the war drew to a close and the resources of the South had been exhausted or destroyed. The lack of warm clothing, blankets, and medical aid created misery for the common soldier. The horror of war, coupled with the agony of sleepless nights on an empty stomach made a Rebel ask who was more fortunate, the dead they buried in mass graves on the battlefield, or those who had to live and fight again.

J. L. Boone of Cleburne was at the battle of Franklin,[1] and the memory of the horror of war still haunted him in 1912 when he wrote:

At Franklin there was the greatest slaughter I ever saw. We went up to Nashville barefooted, worried and disheartened. You could track the boys through the snow by the blood on their feet. The snow was from three to five feet deep. I was detailed to go on vidette[2] duty and refused to go. This was the only time during the war that I refused to obey orders. I was barefooted and decided before I would go out and stand on snow and sleet I would die. I was arrested and sent to the General. I have waded streams when my clothing would

---

1   The campaign of Franklin and Nashville, Tennessee took place from November 29 through December 27, 1864, also known as Hood's Tennessee Campaign.

2   Sentry duty.

freeze on me. It was nothing but the protection of Providence that I am still alive at the age of 73 years.

And **E. R. Boaz of Lindale** recalled that terrible time that seemed to overshadow the hardships he had suffered at Vicksburg:

We followed the Federals to Nashville[3] and had two days fighting. Many men were barefooted. I saw many men take green beef hides and cut out moccasins and sew them on their feet with strings of the same kind.

In northern Arkansas, **Elihu P. Blanton of Cleburne** reported:

I was without shoes part of the time, and during those winters I do not remember sleeping warm but one night, which was some twenty miles above Little Rock and on the night I speak of it was snowing and the weight of the snow on our blanket kept us warm.

Traveling over the mountainous terrain only added to the suffering:

I was on fatigue duty that day with the wagon train, and we had to go up a very steep mountain, and the rain began falling and the water was running down the roadway almost knee deep. We were all day getting to the top. After getting to the top the train was forced to camp. The army had gone on some ten miles and was expecting the train to catch up with them by night, but we did not reach them until the next day about 12 o'clock. There the smuttiest looking men you ever saw, for they had staid around a pine knot fire all night. They could not go to bed as we had their blankets. They had not had anything to eat since the day before and were certainly a hungry set of men.

---

3   Nashville, Tennessee, December 15-16, 1864.

J. C. Boyd of Hawley reported:
I have walked through blood shoe mouth deep when it was running like water.

W. M. Belew of Blue Ridge could not sleep because of the cries of the wounded in the woods at Chickamauga:
At the battle of Chickamauga[4] we fought for three days. We whipped the Yankees and drove them back into Chattanooga. On the second night the leaves burned to death a number of wounded men of both sides. The battlefield lay between the lines. Oh, the horrible cries for help I heard that night from those poor wounded men!

E. W. Beeland of Farmersville fought his first battle in June 1864 and reported on the battle of the Crater:
The mine explosion blew up our battery and the place called "Crater Hill."[5] Grant put a regiment of negroes[6] in front of his white troops and after the explosion they charged us. We killed 1,300[7] in less than an hour. My position as picket gave me a good view of the whole engagement. After the negroes were killed, they were followed by the white troops, many of whom met the same fate, until the "hole" was nearly full of dead men. On Sunday a flag of truce was raised so that we might look after our dead and wounded, and as this relieved me from my post as picket, I was allowed to go over the battlefield. I was very hungry and I found

---

4   Battle of Chickamauga, September 19 and 20, 1862.

5   Battle of the Crater, Petersburg, Virginia, July 30, 1864.

6   Brig. General Edward Ferroro's division of black troops had been trained to spearhead the assault, but some reports say Meade and Grant ordered Burnside to substitute a division of white soldiers for political reasons.

7   Union casualties were 3,798.

*enough food in haversacks of dead men to give me the first
square meal I had had in six months.*

T. H. Stewart of McGregor was also at the Crater and gives
this view:

*At the "blowup" at Petersburg we lost heavily. Many who
were not killed in the explosion were covered up to their
waists in dirt, and the negro soldiers beat them over their
heads with their guns.*

L. N. Perkins of Plainview could have probably found plenty
of food in the haversacks at Gettysburg if he wanted to look:

*My first great battle was that of Chancellorsville,[8] when I
was but a little over eighteen years of age. I came out unhurt,
though my hat brim was shot off, and my comrades on each
side of me were wounded. When we went into Gettysburg the
battle had been raging for two days, and we marched over the
ground which had been occupied by Gen. Pickett.[9] There were
places where one could have walked hundreds of yards on the
bodies of the dead—blues and grays together—without ever
touching the ground. At one place an old railroad cut was
completely blocked with dead bodies.*

John Ashton of Mabank:

*In the battle of Mansfield[10] we charged the enemy through
an old field. They stood until we were in fifteen steps of them
and then they fell back to Pleasant Hill. The loss was very
great. I passed back by there the next day and saw the place
where our comrades were buried. They were buried in
trenches with their hats and clothes on. We were on this one*

8   Chancellorsville, Virginia, May 4, 1863.

9   George Edward Pickett.

10   Mansfield, Louisiana, also Pleasant Grove, Sabine Cross Roads, April
     8, 1864.

raid for some four or six weeks, and during that time never undressed. . . . The way we washed our clothes was to wrap up in a blanket and go to a pond or river and rub them the best we could without soap. . . . . . I well remember standing picket in a bottom. It was sleeting and snowing. I built me a brush pile to stand on in order to keep out of the water. I had to stay there for two hours, and when the sergeant came to relieve me I wrapped up in a blanket and, lying down on the pile of brush, went to sleep. I slept for four hours and then had to stand for two hours more.

B. W. Bailey of Flo recalled the battle of Chickamauga:[11]

On the 19th and 20th of September we had one of the hardest battles that was ever fought on Confederate soil. We gained the battle, but paid very dearly for it. It is said that we lost thirty thousand[12] men, killed, wounded, or missing. I have seen dead men on the ground so thick that you could not walk without stepping on them.

S. O. Adams of Floydada, who was discharged because of age but reenlisted as soon as possible, gives us some idea of the carnage of battle:

My command at Malvern Hill[13] charged across a field 600 yards and captured thirty-two pieces of artillery. The scene was awful. There were six or eight horses to the wagon all down in a pile, some dead and some wounded; with dead and wounded men mixed in with them. After the battle we went to Garrett's[14] farm on June 27, 1862. There were three

---

11 Chickamauga, Georgia, September 19-20, 1863.

12 Reports show Confederate losses at 2,312 dead, 14,674 wounded, and 1,468 missing. Federal losses were 1,657 killed, 9,756 wounded, and 4,757 missing.

13 Malvern Hill, Virginia, July 1, 1862. Also known as Crew's Farm or Poindexter's Farm.

companies off on picket duty, which left us with about 1,000 men. However, we opened the ball about 3 p.m. and staid in the fight until 10 o'clock that night. We had roll call the next morning and found we had sixty-three whole men, and with this number we formed a battle line and captured eight lines of breastworks.

R. H. Cooke of Wellington fought at Tupelo,[15] Mississippi:

On this march we had but little to eat but parched corn and were barefooted and were compelled to march through the ice and snow at Shoal Creek had to wade through the water three feet deep for four hundred yards.

John Overton Casler of Oklahoma City experienced one of the more horrible results of man's inhumanity to man:

Our Pioneer Corps then went to work burying the dead, when I witnessed the most horrible sight my eyes ever beheld. On the left of our line, where the Louisiana Brigade had fought the last evening of the battle, and where they drove the enemy about one mile through the woods, and then in turn fell back to their own position, the scene beggars description. The dead and badly wounded from both sides were lying where they fell. The woods, taking fire that night from the shells, burnt rapidly and roasted the wounded men alive. As we went to bury them we could see where they had tried to keep the fire from them by scratching the leaves away as far as they could reach. But it availed not; they burnt to a crisp. The only way we could tell to which army they belonged was by turning them over and examining their clothing where they lay close to the ground. There we would usually find some of their clothing that was not burnt, so we could see

---

14 Garnett's Farm, Virginia, June 28, 1862.

15 Tupelo, Mississippi, July 14 and 15, 1864.

whether they wore the blue or the gray. We buried them all alike by covering them up with dirt where they lay. It was the most sickening sight I saw during the war and I wondered whether the American people were civilized or not, to butcher one another in that manner; and I came to the conclusion that we were barbarians, North and South alike. Here our loss was estimated at ten thousand five hundred; the enemy's at eighteen thousand,[16] but we lost Gen. Jackson[17] who was a whole corps in himself.

According to **R. W. Reaves of Mount Vernon**, a Confederate officer saved some Federal wounded from being burned:

At the battle of Chicamauga, after fighting on Saturday, the battle renewed Sunday morning by the Confederates advancing. We drove the Federals from their position in such confusion that they did not have time to remove their wounded. A part of Gen. Thomas' [Federal] army took position on some hills and my regiment, Col. G. D. Johnson's was sent along in the evening to dislodge him. In our march we found quite a number of wounded Federals. The artillery had set the woods on fire and they were liable to be burned. Col. Johnson halted the regiment and had them all removed to an old field, where they would be out of danger of the fire. We then renewed our advance and in less than ten minutes we were under fire again. I mention this to show the humane character of the Southern soldier under trying circumstances.

Burton Conerly of Marshall witnessed a burning of the wounded at Spotsylvania:[18]

---

16   Union losses at Chancellorsville were listed at 1,606 killed, 9,762 wounded, and 5,919 missing. Confederate losses were 1,665 killed, 9,081 wounded, and 2,018 missing.

17   Thomas Jonathan "Stonewall" Jackson.

The ground in front of us was covered by the dead and wounded Yankees, and the pine straw and leaves caught fire from the exploding shells, and long lines of fire lighted the woods and burned over the dead and wounded. The flashes of the exploding cartridge boxes on the dead and wounded could be seen as the long sweep of flame went over them and the cries of the wounded for help, which could not come, was something heart rending. Our ambulance corps did what it could, and rescued many from death, at the peril of their own lives.

Conerly heard the men crying, "Lee to the rear," as the general had come to within fifty yards of the front, and soon the fog and smoke-covered battlefield became a slaughterhouse:

On the right, where the enemy was still in our trenches, the fighting was close and deadly, while the charges made on us in front came to hand to hand conflicts, in spite of our rapid firing with so many guns. The enfilading[19] fire from our right, where the men were fighting across the "traverses" would have made our position untenable had not the "traverses"[20] protected us. There was an incessant stream of rifle balls passing over us as well as hundreds of exploding shells. The rain poured down upon us in torrents, and the ditches were filled with water, reddened by the blood which flowed from the dead and wounded. We were forced to sit or stand on the bodies of the dead, covered with water.

And even the landscape and the dead were not spared the horror of war:

---

18 Spotsylvania, Virginia, May 7 through 20, 1864.

19 Gunfire directed from the side of a line of troops.

20 Probably sunken paths in the terrain that offered cover to the men.

The trees in our rear were shot to splinters. One, eighteen or twenty inches in diameter, fell from the constant pelting of the minie balls and shells, while the bodies of the dead which lay in exposed positions were riddled beyond recognition.

When the ordeal was finally over, Conerly reported:

About daybreak we withdrew from our position, the enemy also having retired from our front. With blackened faces and crisped hands, from being in the water so long; our clothing stained with red mud and blood, we marched out of this place where more than one-third of our men lay dead to sleep forever.

But even after the battle was over and the dead buried, there could be no peace, according to **G. B. Scroggins of Winfield**:

After the battle of Manassas, about the 21st of August, following, I visited the battlefield and saw the markers showing where Gen. Bee of South Carolina fell as well as others. Some of the mounds where the slain were buried had been washed down by the rains and exposed here and there was a hand or a foot.

Miles A. Dilliard of Blossom, who had taken a shot through his beard at Murfreesboro,[21] gave an account much like many others who fought in Tennessee in the winter:

On our retreat from Perryville,[22] Kentucky we were ordered to Knoxville, Tennesee. It was snowing and we had but one tent and that was occupied by the medical department. We had men without shoes, coats, hats, and I do not suppose that we had more than a dozen blankets in the regiment. We marched out on a ridge where the young timbers

---

21 Murfreesboro (Stone's River), Tennessee, December 31, 1862 through January 2, 1863.

22 Perryville, Kentucky, October 8, 1862.

had grown up and the leaves were still on them, the boys went to building arbors and fires.

W. H. Dubase of Mount Pleasant gave a horrible description of the dead:

I was in the battle of New Hope Church.[23] *I could have walked on dead men for a mile.*

Louis Spence Flatau was living in St. Louis, Missouri, when Miss Yeary collected the memoirs, but he was born near **San Augustine, Texas**. Flatau was one of the few who gave a lengthy, sometimes rambling report on his experiences, but his recollection of the battle of Franklin[24] is the most graphic:

They opened fire first, and that seemed to echo the command from one end of our line to the other to charge. This line gave away at once, and what few of them were left went into the main line. We were then within 600 yards of the muzzles of their guns, when the most terrific infantry and artillery fire that ever swept a field, cut us down by the hundreds. This carnival of death had no more effect in daunting the courage of those wonderful soldiers than if it had been a Fourth of July celebration. Nothing but a bullet would stop them.

His report, perhaps enhanced by the years of telling, still is a grim reminder of the toll of death and suffering the soldiers endured by direct charges against a fortified enemy position:

Our division went over the works in seven places, and every man that went over was killed, except Gen. Gordon.[25] *The ditch in front of the Yankee works was almost filled with dead and dying. Wounded men who fell into this ditch were*

---

23 New Hope Church, Georgia, May 25 through 27, 1864.

24 Franklin, Tennessee, December 16, 1864.

25 George Washington Gordon.

buried by other men climbing the breastworks pushing the dirt down upon them, the dead already being three and four deep, one on top of the other.

And according to Flatau, even the earth suffered:

The ground was torn with bullets and shot as though a harrow had run over it, the dead and wounded were so thick that when the second, third, and fourth charges were made against their works, it became impossible to go forward without stumbling over the dead.

And the dead were perhaps the lucky ones, for there was little hope for the wounded:

No wounded were borne from the field as every litter bearer was shot down. Hundreds of men who fell on the field wounded, were afterwards riddled with bullets from the galling fire that poured from under the enemy's headlog.

The "headlog" provided cover for the Yankees, but not for long:

We shot the headlog entirely away with our small arms, showing the cool, deliberate marksmanship of that wonderful command of veterans, and nearly every dead and wounded Yankee behind those works was shot in the face or somewhere in the head.

And it only got worse:

They kept up this galling fire until 12:00 at night, holding their line while the main body retreated across the river towards Nashville. The enemy kept up this galling fire from their works, killing hundreds of our wounded that still lay upon the ground in their front of that cold, bitter night. Hundreds of our men bled to death and were frozen to death because they could not be removed. Will any one that was there ever forget the groans and cries of those men who were wounded and freezing and bleeding, to their comrades to come and get them? I was in a squad who volunteered to go to their relief, and we brought the wounded body of Col. Farrell, of the Fifteenth Mississippi, off of the field. The sight that met our eyes the next morning was indescribable. Thousands lay upon that field, dead and dying. You could see squads of these veterans who had fought together, and slept together, kneeling down around the body of some dying comrade, and their grief was so great that they wept like women.

General Hood rode along the line the following morning, and Flatau reported the following:

He was heard to say, with tears streaming down his face, "My poor, poor boys; too bad!" So sure was he that we would be successful in that fight that my battery was equipped like infantry, and we were ordered to charge with Company E of the Fifteenth Mississippi, so as to turn their own guns on them after we had captured them; but what a disappointment, what a mistake? Not a mistake as to the men who were behind these works. Seldom in the war did we ever meet such a set of Americans as we met at Franklin.

At Shiloh, **Chas. W. Geers of Pilot Point** gave a similar horrid picture of the battlefield:

The Confederates and the Federals swept through the camps together. But the Federals sounded the "long roll" and the bugles were calling them to form in line. Hardee swept on and on, until a long line of Federal Infantry, which had formed in the rear of the retreating Federals, met him. This staggered his men for a short time only, but they immediately rushed upon this line also, with such irresistible force that the enemy was beaten back. Ere long they stopped and turned again to "make fight," but were put to the flight again, leaving hundreds of their comrades, in a long line dead upon the field. Hundreds of them were wounded, crawling about like worms, and some calling for water.

By two o'clock, he reported that the ground from the hard rain was deep and red with the blood of men and animals.

W. H. Shook of Ennis, after a day of battle at Manassas Junction,[26] faced an even harder night:

Upon our arrival we found a great many of his men killed and wounded, and the Yankees were gaining the day; but we checked them with a charge about 6 o'clock in the morning. The enemy had about 50,000 men and we had only 18,000. We charged them, killing, wounding and capturing 2,896. We came out victorious about 6 o'clock in the evening. After the battle was over we were ordered to lie down and rest, and I tell you that this is one night that I will never forget as long as I live. We were forced to move the dead before we could find a place to lie down. I could not sleep, and we had no rest for three days and nights, and very little to eat.

It was not the deaths of thousands on the battlefield that haunted **A. D. Dixon of Gainesville** for over forty years, but the death of one Confederate:

The most trying time of my three years service was when I was detailed to help shoot one of our boys. His name was Morgan, a fine young man from Ware County, Ga. The poor fellow got homesick and went home without leave, and for the third offence he was court martialed and sentenced to be shot. I was amongst those who had to shoot him, kneeling with his hand on his coffin; but we had to obey orders.

D. W. Fulton of Van Alstyne was born near Clarksville, Arkansas, and enlisted in the Confederate army at Dallas

---

26 Manassas, Virginia. Battles were fought here July 21, 1861, and August 29-30, 1862.

County as a private in the Sixth Texas Calvary. He first fought Indians, was engaged from Elkhorn[27] to Franklin, but best remembered Spring Hill,[28] Tennessee, and an unusual way to tell the depth of water:

I lost my horse from a shot at Spring Hill, Tenn. After we got back to Benton, Miss. 112 of the boys secured a 90 days furlough home; this was in February or March. We crossed the Yazoo River at Yazoo City. We were all afoot and waded water for seventy-six miles until we got to the highlands of Arkansas. We would keep the tallest man in front, and when he would go out of sight, we would get us a log and float across the deep water.

William F. Glaze of Athens fought in many of the battles in Tennessee and Georgia, but it was at Pine Mountain[29] he experienced a most unpleasant and unusual ordeal:

A man named Fitch of Company G, of our regiment came over to talk to us, and had just sat down under our shade when a shell exploded over us and a piece of shell striking the pole glanced down and killed him. It cut the back of his head entirely off.

M. F. Holbrook of Longview witnessed another horrible death:

There were 30,000 Federals at Brownsville, and we moved down the river until within about thirty miles of Brownsville, where we met them and had one small fight. A Captain named Dunn got me to stay with him in a charge on our horses. He was saying in a loud voice, "Charge boys," when the adjutant rode up behind him and told him several

---

27   Elkhorn Tavern, Arkansas, March 7 and 8, 1862.
28   Spring Hill, Tennessee engagement on November 29, 1864.
29   Battles were fought at Pine Mountain, Tennessee, and Pine Mountain, Georgia.

times to halt, but Dunn continued to say "Charge boys." The adjutant said please, Captain, halt, his voice had stopped and I looked to see what was the matter and the blood and brains were spouting from his forehead. A cruel minie ball had done its work and he was falling from his horse.

Martin Vanburen Gribble of Temple was nearly killed or captured due to exhaustion and a wound:

I was wounded in the battle of Perryville,[30] Ky., and Bob Waire was also wounded. He was shot through the mouth and the jaw bone bursted open and the ball passed through, lodging under the skin in the back of the neck. About the second or third day after the battle Bob found me lying under an apple tree in the orchard. I had not been on my feet since being hauled there. Bob said to me, "Mart, you must get up from there." I told him that I could not get up. He went away and returned with a plow handle and a walking stick. He and John Gribble assisted me upon this handle as a crutch and placed the stick in my hand. Bob said that we must go over the battlefield. We started and I assure you that we went very slowly. We got over the battlefield and found our Captain lying by a log near a little house, and there I sat down. Bob wanted to go further, but I was tired, and told him that I could go no further, so he went away and left me. In a short time four or five cavalry men came up at full speed over the dead, as our dead had not been buried. They said to me, "What are you doing here?" I replied that I was just sitting on the log. "Have you been here since the battle?" "No sir, I belong over at the hospital." "To which side do you belong?" "The Confederate." "Who is that lying there?" "My Captain." "What kind of man was he?" "He was a good man and his name was Lambert." They said that he might be a good man,

---

30 Perryville (Chaplin Hills), Kentucky, October 8, 1862.

but was fighting for a bad cause. They said to me, "Whose coat is that you have on?" I replied, "It is mine, I suppose." "No, sir, that is our uniform coat." and it was—but it was all I had. One said to me, "Pull it off." I replied, "Well, if I must, I must," and began pulling it off. Another of the bunch said, "No you will not pull it off." So they got up a quarrel among themselves, and the one who took my part drove them all away from me. But I was sure in my mind that they would come back and kill me, but thanks be to God I have never seen them since. They were all well armed and I had nothing but a plow handle and a walking stick, and was not able to use them in a fight.

M. I. Jones of Dallas missed the actual fighting at Seven Pines,[31] but was not so lucky at Malvern Hill:[32]

Our regiment moved from Mechanicsville to Malvern Hill where on July 1, 1862, we went into that bloody charge about 5 o'clock and fought till after dark. Forty guns of the enemy threw grape and canister into our ranks with terrible effect. Here we charged across an undulating field of about nine hundred yards, and about half way we encountered a deep ravine. This to some extent shielded us from the enemy's batteries. A hot fire now began. We had the advantage as we fired up hill and the enemy down hill and the artillery were unable to depress their guns so as to reach us. Their killed and wounded were left on the field. We buried their dead on July 2, in a drenching rain. The sight of 2,000 dead men, friends and foes, terribly mangled, and lying in rows, was sickening.

---

31 Seven Pines (Fair Oaks), Virginia, May 31 and June 1, 1862.

32 Malvern Hill (Crew's Farm, Poindexter's Farm), Virginia, July 1, 1862.

L. E. Huffman of Crystal Falls seemed to sense the futility of it all:

At Perryville[33] we lost a lot of brave men and accomplished nothing. We arrived at Knoxville on Oct. 23, barefooted, almost naked and literally starved. The next night, the 24th, I had to stand guard barefooted and in the snow six inches deep. So after six weeks of starving and marching and fighting we had accomplished nothing.

Even a post on the Gulf coast offered little relief from the elements, as reported by **John Howard King of Gilmer:**

One night in the winter of 1863 is well remembered by me. We were guarding a port on the Gulf, when five or six of us were sent to guard a bridge. It was very cold, and at the foot of the bridge was an old rifle pit. Someone had rolled off a bale of cotton nearby, and we pulled the bale to pieces, making a bed in the pit and staying there till morning. One poor fellow was missed in the night, in changing pickets, and next morning was found frozen.

John S. Kritzer of Taylor pretty well summed up the lifestyle of the Confederate soldier:

We were poorly clad and poorly fed, living for days on parched corn and drinking swamp water from bayous full of snakes, cypress knees and rotting leaves. Sometimes for a change we had mule meat, and well do I remember on one occasion we were without bread or salt for twenty-one days, and our horses without corn half the time, giving out daily and being turned loose on the prairie, in the woods and in the bogs, to die, and still we did not murmur, but plodded along keeping up as best we could with those who still had horses.

---

33 Perryville (Chaplin Hills), Kentucky, October 8, 1862.

And how did John rate the Yankees?

How long would the Yankees have stood such fare? They would have all deserted and quit the fight. The difference was that we were fighting for our homes and firesides, and they were fighting for pay.

Elbert W. Kirkpatrick of McKinney recalled that the war was not just hard on men:

We marched and camped in all kinds of weather, winter and summer, without shelter. On one occasion more than 100 of our horses froze to death in a single night.

Henry Lacy of Austin witnessed an unusual incident at the battle of New Hope Church:

Near New Hope Church, while we were eating behind a log, one of the men in my company said; "I am going to kill a Yankee as soon as I eat this bread." When he had finished eating he placed his gun on the log and waited. He did not wait long. He raised his head above the log and shot, but the next instance another Yankee sent a ball into his forehead, scattering his brains in every direction. Though he never spoke again, it is strange that he lived two hours in this condition.

B. W. Halcomb of Aspermont found that even an officer could find some good in tragedy:

Dec. 22, 1864 was exceedingly cold weather, spitting snow. I saw where a fire had been near the road and rode out to the old stump, found a few embers and kindled them up. Gen. Hood[34] and escort rode up and asked permission to warm, which was granted, he at the same time making the remark that he had only one foot to get cold.

---

34 General John Bell Hood lost his right leg at Chickamauga.

And when they were able to dodge the shells and minie balls, the soldiers had yet another great enemy, as reported by **A. Schappaul of Bartonville:**

One evening at roll call there were in my company 110 stout men before a battle and only nine were able for duty, and I was one of the nine. The balance were all down with measles, and before winter twenty-five were dead of that dreadful disease, and the next winter the boys had for good measure, yellow janders and the mumps and typhoid fever. I lay quite low with it at Center, Va. in a tent with the snow two feet on a level. I was down four weeks without any more attention and comfort than the other boys.

Snow and disease followed **O. P. Scott of Dallas** on a boat headed for prison, where he had another chilling experience:

After being captured at Arkansas Post[35] we were crowded on boats with a regiment of guards who had smallpox. The first night on board a big snow fell. We were eighteen days on the Mississippi River. We were crowded on deck like sticks and suffered a great deal from the cold. In fact, I got so cold at one time that I got under the blanket with a dead man, but soon found that I could get no warmth there; got out and slipped into the guard room with the men, but when the first relief came I was discovered and barely escaped the point of a bayonet.

J. F. Smith of Morgan gives an account of the inept way most battlefield burials were carried out:

Breaking camp in the spring, we went into Arkansas. We passed the battlefield at Elkhorn[36] and saw the effects of war. Both Federals and Confederates had been hurriedly buried

---

35 Arkansas Post, Arkansas, January 10-11, 1863.

36 Battle of Elkhorn Tavern, Arkansas, March 7-8, 1862.

in gullies and scantily covered, and the recent rains had exposed their skeletons in all their ghastly horrors.

Dr. Frank Rainey of Dallas saw a similar sight:

When we went to the old battlefield of Bisland[37] we saw there a part of Yankee uniforms and scattered about were legs and arms and heads which had escaped from their hastily dug graves.

F. M. Smith of Waco saw a man die, even from a place of relative safety:

At Malvern Hill I saw a man sitting by a tree. A cannon ball had gone through a part of the oak tree and killed him. He had food in his hands and mouth and had been taking a quiet meal. James Taylor was killed at Chickamauga by a shell. I stood behind an oak at the Wilderness which had seventeen balls in it low enough to kill a man.

So many army units were formed from hometowns or counties that heavy losses to an outfit also meant tragic family losses, as reported by **E. C. Wilson of Childress**:

Was wounded twelve times in the third day fight at Gettysburg.[38] Was with Pickett's Division that day. Received two saber cuts on the back of the head, had end of thumb shot off, wounded in knee, and several small wounds. Was in the battles of Gettysburg and Bull Run. At Gettysburg we drove the enemy forty feet and we had a hard hand to hand fight. I lost my father and four brothers that day.

B. H. Tyler of Roscoe, like so many others, could not get the agony of burying the dead off his mind:

---

37 Fort Bisland, Louisiana, skirmish on April 12, 1864.

38 Gettysburg, Pennsylvania, July 3-4, 1863.

Hearing of some reinforcement coming on to Canby, we turned to meet them, which we did at Glorietta,[39] *and gave them another licking. One of my mess was shot dead not more than six feet from me. When he fell I stopped to see if he was dead and then pushed on to avenge his death. Lieut. Col. Scurry was in command that day and he was always in the lead. About the time we raised the yell, and they fled again and the thing was over, and we were called to a halt. And soon we went about gathering up our dead and putting them away, which we did the best we could. We dug a big hole large enough for them and laid them two deep and spread one layer of blankets over them and filled in on them with dirt. It was bad, but the best we could do.*

Elun Hodge Stephenson of Austin had a hard time forgetting the field hospital:

From Knoxville we went to Murfreesboro, fighting most all Christmas week, with heavy fighting on the 30th and 31st of December, 1862. All who were slightly wounded and able to walk were ordered to make it to Shelbyville. We finally went to Chickamauga. We crossed Lee and Gordon's mills. I was wounded on the foot by a piece of shell or hand grenade as we were taking the first line of breastworks. I was carried to the field hospital and my foot was dressed by Dr. E. Latham, who was covered with blood, and a pile of feet, legs, hands, and arms were piled up to the top of the tables and for some yards back.

Bennet Wood of Temple was one of those veterans who wrote a lengthy report on the war and listed several instances that illustrated the cost to both sides:

---

39   Battle of Glorieta Pass, New Mexico Territory, March 26-28, 1862.

My messmate, Whitten, was so torn by grapeshot that he seemed to have no whole bones. The Zouaves who were pitted against the Texas Brigade, I guess, were all killed, for the earth was strewn with them and I never heard of one after that day. If any escaped they changed their big legged pants for another uniform.

David S. Williams of Texarkana gave a vivid account of atrocities:

After the battles of Mansfield and Pleasant Hill, where Banks was defeated by Gen. Dick Taylor, Churchill's and Walker's Divisions made forced marches back to Arkansas to meet Gen. Steele who was marching south from Little Rock. These two divisions with Marmadukes's, Cabell's, and Maxey's Cavalry, met Gen. Steele at Camden, Ark., where he was well fortified. Steele's supplies were cut off on the east by Gen. Fagan and Gens. Cabell and Maxey on the west. He evacuated Camden on the approach of the infantry forces of Walker and Churchill and the next day about forty or fifty miles north we fought the battle of Jenkins Ferry, completely routing Steele's army. During the first part of this engagement our forces had to fall back, but soon rallying, they drove the Federals from the field and across the Saline River. We found that many of our wounded had been mutilated in many ways. Some with ears cut off, throats cut, knife stabs, etc. My brother, A. J. Williams, acting Sergeant Major, was shot through the body, had his throat cut through the windpipe and lived several days. I saw several who were treated in the same way. One officer, can't recall his name, wrote on a bit of paper that his lower jaw and tongue were shot off after the battle was over or during the falling back as referred to above.

Being wounded on the field of battle was bad enough, but **Robert Wright of Madisonville** suffered pain from another source:

I was in all the battles on this side of the Mississippi except the battle at Saline River and Arkansas Post. I went through many hardships, such as marching through water from shoe mouth to knee deep and fighting when I had nothing to eat except parched corn. I was not wounded during the war except by vaccination, which nearly ate my arm off, and a large hole in my breast. It was thought that my arm must be amputated. One day as I was lying under a tree I saw two men talking and I heard one of them called "Doc," and I asked him if he was a doctor, and he said he had been but was a soldier now, and he told me to get some white castile soap and wash my arm with it and sprinkle burnt alum over it. I did so and in a few days was able to take up the line of march. Another time I was left in a fence corner to die, and after staying there all night was taken to a house, and I cured myself by drinking water with black pepper in it.

J. W. Wynn of Plainview was a private in Company F, Eleventh Tennessee Infantry and fought in most of the battles in Tennessee:

Some of the most severe hardships we had to undergo was in standing guard, where we were exposed to the wind, sleet and snow, to say nothing of the danger from rifles of foes lurking behind rocks and bushes, ready to pick us off without warning. Then the hard marches with Bragg into Kentucky in 1862, when I divided my "one biscuit a day" with my brother in the Cavalry, who had nothing. The only sleep we got was in marching four abreast with arms locked. On the retreat from Kentucky we camped at Bears Station, a few miles south of Cumberland Gap. That night there came a four-inch snow and the ground froze hard enough to support loaded wagons. That winter, just before the battle of Murfreesboro we camped in the snow which we raked away and spread one blanket on the ground and covered with another. We waked up next morning in water caused by the heat from our bodies. Our clothes were wet and we stood around our fires to dry them out.

Thomas A. H. Wylie of Pilot Point discovered you could not even trust your comrades:

The fight in the bend of Stone River,[40] commonly known as Devil's Den, was fought by Hanson's Kentucky Brigade and Adams' Louisiana Brigade. Gen. Hanson was killed in this charge. The Federals admitted that there were a hundred cannon playing on us in this fight. After the battle, when we went to get our knapsacks, with our reserve clothing, where we had left them under guard, the guard had run away and someone had stolen everything we had. I had a lot of good warm underclothing which had just come from home, and every piece of it was gone. I was left very thinly clad and barefooted, and was sent to the wagon train. As I was trudging along over the frozen ground a soldier gave me a pair of shoes about three numbers too large, but they were a boon to me.

So much importance is placed on the major battles in the East, we sometimes forget that in little-known places, far away from the fighting that made the headlines, private disasters were taking place. **David Shelton Sessions of Ennis** reports of one such incident in Florida:

---

40   Stone's River (Murfreesboro), Tennessee, December 31, 1862, to January 2, 1863.

My company was at Natural Bridge when sixteen others and I were on outpost duty. Col. McCormick and Lieut. Ellis were in command of us; we were scouts. From two to four of the scouts were killed from ambush almost every week. Lieut. Ellis was killed a short time before the surrender. He and a private by the name of Charley Bailey were ambushed and killed at Migret's Creek, near Jacksonville, Fla., by a squad of negro troops in ambush in a thicket. They were not called upon to surrender till after being shot. Ellis clung to his horse for a hundred yards before he fell, and then pulled his pistol around to his front. He and Bailey took my place that day. Capt. Dickerson afterward caught the squad of negroes and hung them.

And like so many others, **Will Ed. Kelly of Cedar Creek** remembered when Zollicoffer was killed:

Was in the battle of Perryville, Ky., Chickamauga, and Fishing Creek, where Gen. Zollicoffer[41] was killed. One incident came under my observation at the battle of Chickamauga. In the battle we lost one of our best Captains, J. D. Ford. Just as we crossed the Chickamauga Creek I saw him fall dead from a rifle shot. Two of his men carried him off. We lost two of our brave boys here, McBee and Ellis. They were hit by a cannon ball, which tore them to pieces. I helped to get the fragments together.

W. T. Gilley of Atlanta reported on the hardships at Petersburg:

I will say I was always at my post when the call came, and once stayed on the battlefield three days with dying and dead all around me. As for clothes, I did very well, except that I got barefooted. I was in the ditches three months at

---

41   Felix Kirk Zollicoffer of Tennessee.

Petersburg, where I could not raise my head above the ground. Then at night I had to crawl over the works to a hole about thirty or forty paces in front of the breastworks and stay one hour alone. For rations we got two biscuits a day and a piece of boiled beef about the size of an egg. Then I was at the "blow-up" where there were all sizes of guns, from pocket pistol to a 140 lb. mortar, blown into the air.

At the battle of New Hope Church, **A. G. Anderson of Fairfield** recorded a terrible reaping of Yankees:

We had only one line of battle and he had seven. We had no breastworks and these seven lines charged us until we killed and wounded more of them than we had men in our lines. They seemed to be drunk, and line after line would charge us and be cut down. They came so close to us that they endeavored to plant their colors right in our lines, and when the flag would go down another man would raise it again. Many of their men rushed into our lines and were clubbed and bayoneted to death. Our batteries on the left had full play and their destruction was terrible. Taken altogether, this was, considering the unequal numbers, the greatest victory of the war. In fact, we almost annihilated Hooker's corps. The next morning Gen. Johnston stood in front of our company and touched seventeen dead Yankees, and after many of the officers and wounded had been carried away.

Not all of the terrible cost of war was from bullets, as **Richard G. Walker of Graham** reported in his brief memoirs:

We drove Curtis' Army back and took a few prisoners; had some small fights and skirmishes. Here the measles struck the army, and twelve hundred were buried before a drop of rain fell on their graves. I had the measles and came so near dying that the doctor said I had consumption and gave me a discharge and I went home.

W. L. Young of Dallas fought at Gettysburg:

I was First Sergeant. I knew how many guns we had and knew that we went into that battle with 416 men and came out with 67 men unhurt. My regiment took 13 pieces of cannon and held them, but we could have walked on dead men for quite a distance. We had three color bearers killed that day and I had one man killed on each side of me in less time than it takes to write this. I can never forget that day. I have been in many hard fought battles but this was the most heart-rending of any that I ever witnessed.

Rally 'round the Flag, Boys

Communication on the battlefield relied heavily on couriers, and the battle flags served as guides for the masses of men who sometimes became snarled in their own numbers.

But whether it be the Stars and Bars or the regimental banner, every soldier took pride in it and protected it as best he could, even to almost certain death. Flag bearers and officers with shining bars were prime targets for sharpshooters.

Henry M. Garrison of Wolfe City was among the ones who survived being a flag bearer, although he got the position by accident:

At the battle of Manassas,[1] after three color bearers were killed in succession, I picked up the flag and after the battle was promoted to color bearer.

And at Fredericksburg, Garrison proved how precious those colors were:

From here (Martinsburg) we marched 100 miles to Fredericksburg[2] and by this time our regiment had dwindled from a thousand to about 200 men. At Fredericksburg sixty of those were killed and one hundred and five captured. We came out of this fight with just forty-two men in the regiment. Here I received three shots in my right arm and sixteen bullet holes in my clothes, but I saved the colors. I took them from the staff and put them in the bosom of my

---

1   Manassas, Virginia, July 21, 1861, and August 29 and 30, 1862.

2   Fredericksburg, Virginia, December 13, 1862.

shirt after they had been riddled with bullets, but the Yankees did not get them.

W. F. McElyea of Greenville gave testimony as to how the Rebels protected their banner:

At the battle of Mansfield[3] our flag was shot down three times and caught and never reached the ground.

William F. Glaze of Athens witnessed another death by an officer reckless enough to wave the flag:

We arrived at Chickamauga[4] and went into the fight next day, Sept. 19, and fought two days. This was the hardest and most complicated battle I was in during the whole war. We lost one-third of our whole brigade [Gist's] in one charge on Sunday, the 20th. The brigade was commanded on this occasion by Colquitt, of the Forty-Sixth Georgia, being the senior Colonel of our brigade. Col. Colquitt was badly wounded here, and our Third Lieutenant, Evan Morgan, was killed while waving a Confederate flag he had picked up on the battlefield and was leading the advance.

J. T. Hamilton of McGregor reported hand-to-hand fighting for the control of a banner:

I shall relate only one more incident concerning an act of heroism in the battle of Murfreesboro.[5] The Fifth Arkansas deserves the credit for this noble act. I was in the midst of it and an eye witness. In this charge our company and regiment almost had a hand to hand conflict, in fact, our Colonel ordered us to fix bayonets. J. R. Leslie, I believe it was, rushed to the color bearer of a federal regiment and grabbed

---

3   Mansfield (Pleasant Grove, Sabine Cross Roads), Louisiana, April 8, 1864.

4   Chickamauga, Georgia, September 20, 1863.

5   Murfreesboro (Stone's River), December 31 through January 2, 1863.

the flag staff. The Federal being the larger of the two still held on to the staff, so Leslie pulled the top of the staff down, tore the flag off and crammed it in his bosom, but by this time we had the Federals routed.

Chas. W. Geers of Pilot Point gave vivid evidence that the flag, and the bearer, were primary targets:

We went into battle with 285 men and had 126 killed or wounded. My Colonel, William H. Young, had two horses killed under him; our battle flag had fifty-six holes in it and one shell struck it. We had several men killed while carrying it.

M. I. Jones of Dallas was at the battle of Sharpsburg,[6] or as the Federals called it, Antietam:

My regiment went into the fight at Sharpsburg about daylight and was engaged till noon. At Sunken Road the enemy enfiladed our regiment and we were forced to fall back under a terrible artillery fire. Here we had four Color Bearers killed.

L. E. Huffman of Crystal Falls reported that he was living in Charleston and heard the first gun fired at the *Star of the West* when she attempted to provision Fort Sumter,[7] and tells of the heroics of a flag bearer:

At the battle of Bentonville,[8] N.C., the last one in which I was engaged, we charged the enemy and took two lines of breastworks, and followed them to the third, before we noticed that we were entirely separated from the army. Our flag bearer, Ruben Owen, tore the flag from its staff and

---

6   Sharpsburg (Antietam), Maryland, September 17, 1862.
7   Fort Sumter, North Carolina, where the first shot of the war was fired.
8   Bentonville, North Carolina, March 19 through 21, 1865.

stuffed it in his bosom. We all were sent to the rear without being disarmed, and when night came they captured guards, disarmed them and marched them into a swamp, where we remained until we could escape. We would march all night and lay up in the day. The second day we captured a quartermaster and his horse, and got back into camp about noon the next day. We were greeted with cheers as we marched down the lines, triumphantly flying our old flag and bringing in as many or more prisoners than were in our ranks.

Perhaps the most exciting flag incident did not take place on the battlefield, but in prison, as reported by **J. H. Hunter,** who failed in his lengthy report to name his hometown:

The mention of Camp Douglas,[9] even at this late day, carried a shudder among the survivors who experienced the horrors of prison life in that gateway of death during the Civil War. Camp Douglas, Chicago, was a Northern prison. In the garrison square of this prison stood a flag pole twenty-eight inches in diameter at the base and tapering to a diameter of six inches at the top. This flagstaff was 180 feet high and from its lofty summit floated one of the largest of Uncle Sam's banners. Abraham Lincoln was assassinated on the night of April 14, 1865. In token of respect for the late Chief Magistrate of the Nation, the flags of all military posts were ordered lowered to half mast. On the morning of April 15, while attempting to lower the flag at Camp Douglas, the lanyard fouled in the topmost pulley and refused to yield. There were twelve thousand prisoners being held in Camp Douglas at that time these were being guarded by three thousand Federals under the command of Colonel Sweet.

---

9   Federal prison camp at Chicago.

Hunter, along with the other prisoners watched as a Federal soldier began to climb the 180 foot pole, swaying in the Chicago wind:

He was furnished with a belt and gaffs to insure his safety. The entire garrison and many of the imprisoned Confederates watched this soldier as he slowly ascended the lofty shaft of swaying timber, a fierce gale was blowing off the lake and the movements of the climber were slow and laborious. They saw him reach the top, and pause as if to rest. Then they saw him extend a hand overhead as if to replace the lanyard in the pulley, and then they saw him shoot downward as if thrown by a mighty force from that lofty pinnacle. He lived two hours after the fall, which was caused by the breaking of his belt.

Colonel Sweet decided that he would not risk the lives of any more Federals:

"Try the Johnnies," said a subaltern.[10] *"They have been trying to pull that flag down these four long years. Give the Johnnies a chance!"*

It was a happy suggestion and Colonel Sweet acted upon it, with good common sense and decision. He knew that no Confederate prisoner in Camp Douglas would undertake to climb that pole for accommodation or for the entertainment of the spectators. It would require an incentive out of the ordinary to induce one of those twelve thousand cold, hungry and emaciated prisoners to perform a duty that had appalled three thousand well fed, well clad Yankees.

The next day, the flag was still jammed and Sweet told his adjutant to offer five hundred dollars in cash, an immediate

---

10   Any commissioned army officer below a captain in rank.

discharge from prison, and free transportation home to any prisoner who would climb the pole:

Scarcely had he uttered the last words of his sentence, when a lean, lank cadaverous boy, an artillery man, said to have been from Georgia, sprang two paces to the front and saluted the officer, who with his orderly, as one conducted him to the flag pole, where a climber's belt, new and strong, was carefully fitted to his waist and the gaffs adjusted to his ankles.

The crowd waited for the lad to make the climb, some reasoning that he would get his discharge when he hit the ground:

And the ribald jest went around among the Federals, while multiplied thousands of eager upturned faces gazed upon the daring young artillery man from the "Old Red Hills of Georgia" as he slowly, calmly, steadily, ascended to the top of the flagstaff. They saw the towering shaft sway as a reed before the furious wind as he neared the top, and shuddered lest he would make a false move and be hurled to death, as was the unfortunate soldier on the preceding day. But onward and upward he went, and, reaching the top, he was seen to arrange the lanyard and guide it into its proper groove in the pulley. During these latter moments the great multitude below were held under the spell of a profound silence—a silence of dramatic suspense. When the Georgia boy had released the lanyard, for the first time he turned his head and looked down upon the sea of upturned faces. Whether though a spirit of defiance, daring, sauciness, or exultation, no one ever knew, but upon beholding the suspense of the gazing thousands below, he removed his old tattered Confederate hat and threw it at them!

The Rebel yell resounded through Camp Douglas that day, and the boy from Georgia got his five hundred dollars, took the pledge, and went home to Dixie.

E. J. Lake of Lindale was at Gettysburg[11] when he decided he did not want to be just a horse holder:

Thomas Sligh, an Orderly to the Colonel, was told to hold the horses in the rear until called for. Sligh begged to be permitted to go into the battle. During the battle when several flag bearers were killed or wounded, Sligh ran and raised it, when he, too, was soon killed.

C. D. W. McNeil of Port Lavaca had special feelings for the flag:

On April 15, 1865, I was sent to Whitesville, and left orders with a man named Tally to order all militia to report at once at West Point[12] for duty. After eating supper with Mr. Tally I returned to West Point, and made my report to Gen. Tyler[13] at the fort. On getting up I went outside the fort, where Gen. Tyler was eating his last meal on earth, and gave him the military salute. Here Capt. Gonzales said: "Sergeant, how about the flag?" Said I: "Well, by gravy, I forgot to hoist her this morning." So I ran to get the flag, and for the last time hoisted it on the pole. Somehow I could not but admire its beauty, for it seemed to speak these words: "I wave over the true and the brave." I, without thinking repeated along this verse:

"My banner, a simple one, by it I stand;
It floats from the Potomac to the Rio Grande;

---

11 Gettysburg, Pennsylvania, July 1-3, 1863.

12 West Point, Georgia, April 16, 1865.

13 Robert Charles Tyler rose from private to general and lost a leg at Missionary Ridge.

> *Waves over a nation that is gallant and true;*
> *Waves over the Confederacy, my white, red and blue."*

After eating breakfast, I reported to Gen. Tyler for duty, who ordered me to go to town and call for volunteers for the defense of Fort Tyler, and the Southern Confederacy.

McNeal then had an encounter with three small boys, their ages twelve and fourteen, who joined the already dead Confederate cause by "throwing leaden pellets" at the Federal ranks, as "the flag proudly waved over their little heads."

These boys, after seven and three-quarter hours of hard fighting, with their little powder-burned, black faces, surrendered with the rest as prisoners of war, and stood the hardships without a murmur, claiming nothing at the hands of the Yankees. True heroes of the Southern cause. Gen. Tyler refused to surrender the fort and soon the blue line was seen approaching, and my attention was called to the flag. I looked and saw that one of the ropes was cut. I laid down my gun, climbed the pole, repaired the rope, took off my cap and waved it at the Yankees and yelled out, "Hurrah for Dixie. Here's your mule and a one-eyed sorrell one at that," and slid down. Just then Gen. Tyler sent me with six men to guard a bridge, hoping that Gen. Forrest[14] would come to our relief, but he did not come. We were where we could see the fort, and see charge after charge, and finally saw them go over the breastworks, and saw the flagpole fall, which was the last flag to fall east of the Mississippi River.

Not all flag bearers were killed in action, as **William R. Waller of Seymour** explains:

---

14   General Nathan Bedford Forrest of Tennessee.

In an engagement at Bayou Robert[15] the officers deserted their companies and took cover under a bridge. I being the flag bearer, sprang upon the breastworks and ordered the men to "give them hell." The next day the officers failed to respond when going into action, and the men began falling back. I rode to the front and called upon the men to stand firm and turned my attention directly to the enemy. Shot and shell were falling around me. When I turned again to my regiment I found they were running to the woods. I then turned and followed them. On the following day, for my conduct in the fight at Bayou Robert, I was made Captain in the regiment.

As so many others had done, **W. C. Sears of Crowell** carried the flag, even though he knew it made him a prime target for Yankee bullets:

In the spring of 1864, eight corporals were detailed to guard colors, and all were killed or wounded. This left me and one color bearer. He was killed and I took the colors out of his hand. He handed them to me as he fell.

Yank or Reb, carrying the colors was a dangerous position, as **Joseph Mosely of Zulch** proved:

In Louisiana, across the Atchafalaya River, we had been fighting all day without anything to eat, when all at once our army began to retreat, and for about three miles we had to put our horses to their best. I had been separated from my company and dropped behind, but did not know where I was ahead or behind and could not tell for the dust, when presently I turned my horse and looked behind. Suddenly a man rode out in front of me and then a second and then a third, fourth and fifth.... and still I was undecided whether they

---

15   Bayou Robert, Louisiana, a skirmish took place here on May 8, 1864.

were friends or foes until the sixth came out, bearing a Federal flag. I raised my gun and at its fire the flag fell, and I had the opportunity to escape to a canebrake about half a mile away, where some of our men had taken refuge, and where the enemy dared not enter.

Robert Agustus Brantley of Summerville found that a flag can also serve as a defensive weapon:

Rapidly the order was passed down the line, the smoke rising from the Federal works beneath us was so dense that we could not see them, and did not see them until we got beneath it. The old Indian war whoop, now called the "Rebel yell," was raised, and but a few bounds over the dead was made before we were standing at the brink of Pow White Creek and spring, pouring lead into the Federals as rapidly as we could load our guns. We with the flag, landed at the spring, where the gulch began, and the best place to cross the creek. I, without delay, crossed and raised my gun to shoot the first Federal I saw in his works; ran, looking back at me, and some one shot him down. Onderdonk, the color bearer, crossed right behind me and at the same place, Eldredge next. As soon as Onderdonk hit the ground he was shot down and the flag came down at my left. I caught it and looked at him. He said; "Take it, I am shot." I then dropped my gun, drew my sword bayonet, raised the flag above my head with a yell, and moved with all speed for the heights, and when I passed over this wounded Federal he was still looking at me. I was soon at the crest of the hill, nearly 100 yards from my regiment; at the top of the hill were a few tents, and I stopped near one of them, and there stood three officers and two privates talking earnestly; the officers seemed to be looking down the hill with their backs half turned to me, the privates were on the far side of the officers, looking in my direction.

When I ran up and yelled, one of them with an oath said, "There is a d— rebel now," and raised his gun to shoot, and as he did I threw the flag in his face; he fired but did not hit me. After this, they all broke and ran down the hill.

Soloman Thomas Blessing of Fort Worth told of a flag made of unusual material:

On Sept. 17, we fought the battle of Sharpsburg,[16] or as the Federals call it, Antietam. I was in the charge in the corn field and was near our regimental flag when I saw the bearer fall. My first impulse was to pick it up, but then thought I could do more good shooting. This flag was made from the wedding dresses of Mrs. Jefferson Davis and Mrs. Louis T. Wigfall, and presented to the regiment at Camp Wigfall.

The sight of the flag was an inspiring moment for most soldiers, and **Frank Herron of Graham** was no exception, especially if it was being waved by pretty girls:

We arrived at Raymond[17] early in the morning of the 11th of May, 1863, and next morning were ordered out to relieve a company which had been on picket the night before. Without breakfast, tired, hungry and blistered feet, sadness was pictured on the faces of my companions as we were hastening through the dust to death of some of us and to great suffering of others. But our sadness was suddenly relieved when we saw on a porch of a palatial home some beautiful girls waving the "Bonnie Blue Flag." We gave the old and familiar yell in return, and no sad faces were seen for a while, but on the other hand duty to our Southland and our Southern homes, could be seen pictured on the faces of every member of our company.

---

16 Sharpsburg (Antietam), Maryland, September 17, 1862.

17 Raymond, Mississippi, engagement on May 12, 1863.

J. C. ALEXANDER, McGregor

S. T. BLESSING, Fort Worth

Gen. W. L. CABELL

Gen. R. M. GANO, Dallas

J. P. HALE, Farmersville

J. T. HOWARD, Farmersville

JAMES H. MATHIS, Dallas

H. A. MOREHEAD, McGregor

JOHN MURCHISON, Farmersville

Gen. FELIX H. ROBERTSON

H. M. ROLLINS, Farmersville

L. A. SALLEE, Del Rio

A. J. SEWELL, McGregor

J. H. SMITH, McGregor

T. H. STEWART, McGregor

JAS. K. P. YEARY, McGregor

Hardtack and Rats

At the beginning of the conflict, there was an abundance of food in the South, but as the war continued this diminished after thirty or forty thousand men moved over the terrain like a swarm of locusts, devouring everything the populace could not find a place to hide. And a hungry belly finally reached the point where just about anything that came close to being edible was welcome.

E. R. Boaz of Lindale fought his first engagement at Port Gibson[1] May 1, 1863, and was at Baker's Creek[2] May 16. But his most vivid memories were of the siege of Vicksburg:[3]

Was in the siege of Vicksburg forty-eight days. Ate mule beef and pea bread, my self and two others ate mule's head without bread. I got hungry enough to eat green persimmons.

Z. McDonald of Jonesboro was another Vicksburg survivor who learned to appreciate mules:

We were near the end of the siege now, and hunger was telling on us. So some one introduced mule beef. At first I made up my mind that I would not eat any of it, but finally I decided to taste it and found it would appease hunger, and that was what I needed, so afterwards I took all I could get.

---

1 Mississippi, May 1, 1863.

2 Mississippi, May 16, 1863.

3 Mississippi, October 16 through December 20, 1862.

J. C. Boyd of Hawley fought at Chancellorsville[4] and Petersburg,[5] where his mealtimes were either feast or famine:

At the battle of Chancellorsville we fought four days and nights without food. While on a charge we ran the Northern soldiers and while going through where their quarters had been, I ate the largest meal of my life. I was a sharpshooter at the time Petersburg was blown up. We found where the Federals had fed their horses and picked up corn from the ground and ate it. I thought it was about as good eating as I ever had. We fought the next day without anything to eat until just before night, when our food was brought to us. The food consisted of raw hog jaws with the hair on. We took our knives and scraped the hair off as best we could and ate the meat off the bone. I had hardtack with it.

John Ashton of Mabank, in the battle of Mansfield,[6] spoke of the unusual diet the soldiers sometimes had to endure:

We dodged around the river bottom for two days and nights without anything to eat. The next day we found a poor pig, killed, broiled and ate it. The third day we got out to a house. I went to the gate and the lady brought me out some coffee and sweetbread and I could not keep it on my stomach.

John R. Baker of Amarillo found prison food to be somewhat less than appetizing:

Was taken prisoner on the 23rd day of February, 1864, and sent to Fort Delaware.[7] Remained there until March 8, 1865. There were 14,000 prisoners in this prison at one time.

---

4   Chancellorsville, Virginia, May 2-4, 1863.

5   Petersburg, Virginia, July 30, 1864.

6   Louisiana, April 8, 1864. Also known as Pleasant Grove or Cross Roads.

7   Built on Pea Patch Island in the Delaware River, it was the most dreaded of Federal prisons.

Rations of about one-half loaf of bread and two ounces of meat per day, and all the rats we could catch.

George C. Baker of Rosenberg pretty well summed up the quest for food and the joy of receiving it:

At the battles of Harrisburg and Tupelo[8] we were engaged for seven days and nights, and four of these days we were without food. At the end of that time we were issued three day's rations and we consumed it all at one meal.

P. G. Beauchamp was born in Georgia, but moved to Daingerfield, Texas, with his family in 1856 and in 1912 was living in **Collinsville**:

We were on this raid two months—December and January—and came near freezing several times. Were without anything to eat eight days at one time except of two Indian ponies and some buffalo hides. We looked like we had been through a spell of sickness, but with plenty to eat we were soon all right again.

W. T. Bell of Oakwood was taken prisoner and exchanged, then chose a very poor time to rejoin the Confederate army at Petersburg:

Was again taken prisoner at Farmville[9] on April 6th and marched by the enemy eight days. All the rations we had was a little parched corn and green beef without salt and no way to cook it.

W. R. Bell of Blossom gave an indication of how low a soldier would go for something to eat:

At Newbury Church there was another hard fought battle … our clothing was entirely insufficient and we had little or

---

8   Harrisburg and Tupelo, Mississippi, July 14 and 15, 1864.

9   Farmville, Virginia, engagement April 5 to 7, 1865.

nothing to eat. We drew corn for our rations the same as horse or mules, and had the privilege of eating it raw or parching it.

Some traditional Southern food even seemed to have healing powers as **A. G. Anderson of Denton** reported:

During our stay at Camp Douglas[10] my brother Z. J. Anderson had fever, but we did not allow him to go to the hospital, and with the help of a young doctor we pulled him through, though at one time it seemed he was sure to die. Just as the fever left him, we were ordered to Vicksburg to be exchanged, and he was about to be left when the boys agreed to help me carry him on a cot. We were separated on the boat, but I found him on our arrival at Vicksburg, and we stopped on the sidewalk, not sure what to do, when he spied a watermelon. He begged piteously for some, but I was afraid to allow him to eat it, but finally consented, and he began to improve from that day. No one ever enjoyed anything as much as he did that melon.

Food and females were the downfall of **James F. Byrd of Robert Lee**, who along with his friends, was captured by the Yankees at Fort Pillow:[11]

I will now endeavor to give you a sketch of my capture and escape from the Yankee prison. There were a number of us who had been detailed as scouts to see what we could find out, and had not gone far until we located the Yankees. We stopped on the north side of Pearl River to stay until night and then we intended going over and making a thorough investigation. Lieut. Dick Johnson, ranking as Captain, with part of the men took the horses back across the hill to

---

10   Camp Douglas Prison, Chicago, Illinois.

11   Fort Pillow, Tennesee, April 12, 1864.

feed them and left us to keep a lookout. We had orders not to cross the river, but the temptation was so great that we could not resist as there were some girls who lived just over the river who came down and talked with us, saying they would cook our dinner and bring it over to us if we would not come over to the house. So five or six of us decided that we would go over and take dinner with them. Some of us would stand guard while the others ate, and while on guard looked up the road and saw the Yanks coming; notifying the boys who were eating. We succeeded in getting into the swamp, and if it had not been for a negro woman reporting us we would have succeeded in getting away, but we were forced to surrender.

Benjamin Harrison Daugherty of Chillicothe, like most of the others, remembered the ample supplies of corn, which was parched, eaten raw, or made into hominy, but on one occasion he had an extra delicacy:

We were of course on many long marches, and at one time were without food for three days, and once we had only parched corn to eat two or three days, and one time only goober peas.

J. A. Carver of Temple ate what he could get but didn't have to like it:

Was in the siege of Vicksburg,[12] *where our rations consisted of peas and corn, and very scanty at that. I ate it and would have been glad to have had what was thrown to the dogs back home.*

Every Confederate trapped in the siege of Vicksburg had something to say about the food, or lack of it, and **J. F. Hardy of Marlin** was no exception:

---

12   Vicksburg, Mississippi. First campaign, October 16 through December 20, 1862. Second campaign, April 1-4, 1863.

I laid in the breastworks at Vicksburg, Miss., for forty-eight days and nights without shelter; took the weather like a brute, and ate mule meat and bread made of peas.

And the menu didn't improve much after he was captured and put in prison:

We got a pint of soup and a third of a loaf of bread about 9 o'clock for our breakfast, and about 4 o'clock in the afternoon we would get the same amount of rations for our dinner and supper.

Also at Vicksburg **H. McMullen of Wainsboro** became accustomed to his strange diet, even liked it:

Our bread was made of a mixture of corn and peas raked up from old piles and ground together. How a man's taste will change, or perhaps the women don't know how to cook anyway. The pork and venison we have to eat today is not nearly as good as the mule meat was then.

Dr. James Daniel Callaway of Goldthwaite suffered in Fort Delaware prison but had one delightful meal:

We went through much suffering, but the worst was the two months of starvation at Fort Delaware. My mess killed the house cat of the Lieutenant commanding, and we cooked and ate it. This was the best meal I had during my eight months of imprisonment.

James E. Fitzgerald of Strip was only sixteen years old when he left his family to fight for the South in 1862:

Well do I remember when we were issued one-half of an ear of corn as rations. I threw my part away, thinking that if I could get no more, this would do me no good, but someone told me that I had better keep it. It would taste good before I got any more, and it was only too true.

T. H. Ellison of Lockhart spent most of the war in the eastern theater, but he got a pleasant surprise when he was transferred to Galveston, Texas, in 1864:

Sweet potatoes and oysters were our bill of fare, and not a bad one.

J. F. Freeman of Forney did not fare nearly as well:

Food was very short, so short that we had to eat all the rats and dogs that we could get hold of in order to sustain life and hundreds of boys starved to death.

Not only did **S. T. Honnall of Van Alstyne** recall the biggest fight he was in, but remembered what he had for lunch, too:

The worst battle I was in was at Jackson, Miss., on July 8th and 9th, 1863. We were outnumbered five to one, but we gained the field and buried our dead. My dinner that day was green peas and bacon rinds. This was the first thing I had eaten in four days.

G. R. Howard of Dallas talked about the "best woman I ever saw (except my wife)":

After we had crossed the Cumberland Mountains and had nothing to eat in three days, except a little parched corn, we stopped at a house and begged for something to eat. The woman said, "There is the table. Help yourselves if you can find anything to eat." The soldiers who just finished had just about eaten her out. So we sat down to a table with nothing on it except corn bread crusts. You may be sure we demolished them. They were the best bread crusts I ever saw and in fact it looked like she was the best woman I ever saw (except my wife).

Hungry men will eat anything that even looks good, as **Rowland W. Hudson of Farmersville** relates:

Was captured by Gen. Wilson's forces at Selma, Ala., on April 2; was marched to Columbus, Ga., and paroled. We left Selma Sunday night, April 9, and got nothing to eat until Thursday evening, except for raw beef and flour. We made dough with plain water and baked, or rather dried it on rails before the fires. On our march from Selma to Columbus, the roadside being lined with wild roses, which were in bloom, we went for them like cattle for grass. Our stomachs had passed the stage of hunger and turned to nausea. Many of the boys sank down by the wayside.

L. E. Huffman of Crystal Falls found the capture of food as important as catching Yankees:

At Munfordsville[13] we captured a garrison of about 4,800, and at Camp Dick Roberson we captured a good lot of pickled pork and hard tack.

But **H. W. Hunt of Nocona** had a sweeter time. Born in Bonham in 1849, he was only twelve years old when the war started:

I was in no battles, but rode government mules awfully hard. I drew all my rations in sugar, so I had a sweet time during the war.

Food was always a concern, even when there was plenty, and the soldiers took no chances on wasting any of it, according to **W. H. Jones of Brady**:

From Missionary Ridge we went to Dalton and remained till 1864. One morning we had orders to prepare three day's rations which was unusual, but any of us could have eaten it at one meal, which some did, saying "let every day provide for itself," others saying if they were killed they would still have it.

---

13   Seige of Munfordsville, Kentucky, September 14 to 17, 1862.

J. H. Knox of Eolian returned from Price's raid with the fifteen men who were left out of his unit of 500 men, and he was happy to be back in Texas:

We retreated fighting day and night, without anything to eat, and no rest. Many of my comrades were lost and have never been heard from till this day. Then we marched back through Indian Nation to Texas, and crossed Red River. We were almost starved to death. Oh, the good women of Fannin County. They kept their tables set all day, their servants cooking, and all we had to do was to go in, sit down, eat and move on. May the good Lord bless the good women who were in Fannin County in 1864.

Back in Indian Nation, the fare had not been so abundant, or tasty:

I traveled twenty-one days through the Indian nation on foot, as my horse had given out, and in all this long walk I did not have one mouthful of bread. Somewhere in the Nation, late one evening, the command stopped for the night. Major Rayburn, Col. Davies, Capt. Allen, Capt. Hacker, two or three others and myself decided we would go ahead of the command, in search of something to eat. We had gone about two miles when we found an old, broken-down army mule standing by the roadside. Capt. Hacker had given out. We placed him astride the mule, tied a rope around the mule's neck, and one led while two whipped him along. After a while we came to water, and shot the old mule down, skinned out his hams, and we all ate heartily of "Mule Ham."

Probably every military unit in the history of man has had a Zack Sanders, as reported by **Tyre Hancock of Dallas:**

Zack Sanders was another fine forager and afraid of nothing. Zack and I went out one evening and found a fine bunch of sheep grazing near a briar thicket. My gun brought down a fine fat one, and Zack pulled it into the thicket quick. The next day we had the finest baked mutton you ever saw. Joe Ware, our mess-mate, said he was going to ask Lieutenant O. M. Airhart to dinner. We tried hard to get him not to do so, as that particular lieutenant was very hard on foragers, but Joe went and told him that we had a fine beef roast, and the boys all wanted him to take dinner with them. He came, and as we were all seated around the fire and viewing the fine baked mutton he said, "Boys, those are mighty small beef bones," and began talking rather ugly, but Joe Ware said, "Now Lieutenant, we asked you here to eat, and not to make remarks; now, you just eat," and the lieutenant did eat until we were almost sorry we had invited him.

Another officer decided he could bend the rules to feed his hungry troops, as reported by **John Loughridge of Farmersville:**

When Gen. Hood[14] started back to North Georgia, the orders were very strict against straggling and foraging. In fact, Sherman[15] had left but little to forage for; but one old fellow near Altoona had crept back to his old home, built a cabin in place of the house which Sherman's burners had destroyed, split some rails and planted a patch of corn, and the roasting ears were just about ripe. Now a hungry Confederate soldier had no conscience and no fear of punishment, and no sooner had the sun set than there was a crowd of hungry soldiers in his patch, helping themselves. The crowd was arrested and carried before the Major; each holding on to his armful of corn. "Where did you get the corn?" was the question, and "What are you going to do with it?" "Over there," indicating the direction, and "am going to eat it." The

---

14   General John Bell Hood.

15   Union General William Tecumseh Sherman.

Major's heart was with the boys, but we must have discipline. "Put it down and retire to your command" was the stereotyped questions and replies, till at last the pile had grown to considerable size, when one man was asked what he was going to do with the corn, replied, "going to place it on the pile and retire to my command." The Major turned to the old fellow and said, "Old man, I can't do anything with a hungry soldier." Then the scramble began. Each one wanted his contribution to the pile, and just a little more.

Roasting ears was one of the more abundant of foods, and even a battle could not stop the Confederate soldier from dining on them, as in the memoirs of **R. B. Neely of Olney**:

Was in the battle of Raymond,[16] Miss., Chickamauga,[17] and in the great struggle of 100 days from Dalton to Jonesboro,[18] Ga. At this battle I had some roasting ears in my haversack and the boys tried to get me to throw them away, but I carried them in the charge and was wounded in the cheek within twenty steps of the enemy, but rallied. Ate my roasting ears on picket that night.

George W. O'Neal of Wolfe City found that when foraging for food, not all money talked:

Were stopping in Maryland for a few days, I thought that I would go out while we were in the country and secure some butter, bread, and milk, if possible. So I approached an old fashioned residence and halted at the entrance. A lady made her appearance and as I was explaining to her my mission a gentleman made his appearance and asked me what I wanted and what I was doing there. I explained to him the

---

16 Raymond, Mississippi, engagement on May 12, 1863.

17 Chickamauga, Georgia, September 19-20, 1863.

18 Jonesboro, Georgia, August 31 to September 1, 1864.

object of my visit and also told him that I was not trying to steal anything; neither was I begging, but I wanted something to eat and had the money to pay for it. He said that he was very well supplied with Confederate money. I then told him that I would pay him with greenback. He then wanted to know how much greenback money I had. I told him that I had $20.00, and he became very much interested about my affairs and wanted to make a trade with me and told me that he would give me forty Confederate money for my twenty dollars in greenback, and the bread and butter and milk in the bargain. I told him that trade suited me exactly. He loaded me up with the butter, light bread, and milk and gave me the forty dollars and I gave him my twenty and went on my way rejoicing.

W. J. Ridings of Graham was more concerned with the color of the food than the quantity, and he had a special problem that complicated mealtime:

On our march from Tennessee into Kentucky our rations gave out. Our biscuits were made of bran and flour mixed together, and we had two ears of corn issued to each man at night. As I had not teeth it was hard for me to eat it, and the beef was not much better. It was "Longhorn" and very blue.

Corn seemed to be the common ingredient in every Confederate diet, but it could get old, as noted by **W. J. Rutledge of Kenedy:**

It would be hard to tell of all the hardships we went through during the four long years of fighting and marching day and night. I have walked till my feet were blistered, and then on other occasions I would freeze, and then starve, and if it was not one thing it was something else and more of it. Parched corn is good for lunch after supper around the fire

on a cold night, but when it comes to eating one ear a day, it
ceases to be funny.

At the siege of Vicksburg, bringing in a special meal took
courage, coupled with a little deception, as **A. J. Sewell of
McGregor** reported:

*We had a ditch out from our main ditch to the spring
from which we carried water. We had our pickets out through
this ditch. There were three or four hogs that got to coming
around our outpost. Now, our sentinel and the boys were
very anxious to get them, but how to get them without alarm-
ing the camp was the question. The men finally decided that
as I was the smallest one in the company I should be put on
guard on the outside post and was to shoot the hogs. In a
short time they came and I shot them. Instantly the officer of
the day was on the spot and our part of the army was ready
for action. The officer of the day inquired the cause of the
shooting, and my answer was, "There was something out
there." Finally everything quieted down. We then carried the
hogs into the ditch, dressed them and divided with the other
boys. We had a regular feast, but had to be very quiet about it.*

Francis Freeman Scott of Blooming Grove had a more
unusual meal:

*We went to the farm house and as the house was crowded
went to the dairy and for the first time took, without invita-
tion, what did not belong to me. I found a churn of cream
and did not wait for a spoon but used my hands and it was
good. Just as I began an old lady came in and threw up her
hands and said: "Oh, don't eat up all my cream." "I won't,"
said I. There was a five gallon churn full.*

Another strange diet was that of **John T. Poe of Longview:**

*I have subsisted five days at a time on brown sugar,
which we took from the sugar houses in Louisiana. Have*

lain for four days and nights in line of battle with only one meal a day, and that brought in coffee sacks and turned out on the bark of a tree instead of plates. Have gone without water on the Western plains till our eyes sank way back, our tongues swelled, our brains reeled, and many fell by the way, to be relieved when water was found. We who were afoot lived two weeks on mule meat and rabbits, just as we could shoot them on the prairies.

Unusual diets were common, but sometimes something was missing in the preparation of food, as reported by **Thomas J. Stirman of Richmond:**

I joined Gen. Price's Army near Union, Mo., some forty miles west of St. Louis, and was assigned to duty in Col. A. W. Slayback's Regiment, Shelby's old Brigade and Shelby's Division, and was in all the principal engagements for that famous raid from Jefferson City to Newtonia,[19] Mo. While on detached service near that town I was wounded three times and left for dead. For four days and nights I lay in the woods and never heard a human voice. It snowed the second night after I was wounded, and I killed a raccoon and ate him raw.

But he was not the only Confederate to dine on rare cuisine, as **J. M. Thompson of Belton** tells in his memoirs of a meal he had after the battle of Pleasant Hill:[20]

In this charge we lost our gallant Colonel and many other men. Both sides claimed victory but we drove them two miles from the field when night came on and ended the conflict. It was my misfortune to stand picket on the battle field that night, and of all the duties of the war this was the most

---

19   Newtonia, Missouri, October 28, 1864.

20   Pleasant Hill, Louisiana, engagement on April 9, 1864.

heartrending. During the campaign I had no food for four days and the first food was raw bacon without bread.

J. J. Amason of McGregor went to war believing:

The Yankees could not shoot, and that it would only be like killing squirrels, and we knew what we could do at that.

And at Jackson,[21] Mississippi, they had a "squirrel shoot," picking Yankee sharpshooters out of apple trees. But after laying pinned down for most of a day, laying flat on the ground, that night they were able to build some breastworks for protection:

We had some rest till night, fell back, built some breast-works and staid there until we ate up sixty acres of roasting ears.

Richard Johnson Barbour of Normangee had no trouble finding food, except that some of it tried to bite back:

I was a good forager and when hogs would try to bite me I would kill them and carry them to camp.

Real coffee and bread seemed to be missed by the soldiers most, and **Edward L. Byers of Madisonville** got both at the same time:

We had no dinner that day, and after nightfall with two of my messmates, I went to the camp of Gen. Green,[22] who gave us come coffee and lightbread. And of all the suppers that it has been my lot to share, that one by the light of the camp fire on the banks of the Atchafala[23] will be remembered as the best.

---

21 Jackson, Mississippi, engagement on May 14, 1863 and siege from July 10 to 16.

22 General Thomas Green of Virginia.

23 Atchafalaya River in Louisiana.

At Lookout Mountain,[24] **A. B. Foster of Comanche** did not fare so well, and neither did the officers' horses:

Our rations were so short that we stole corn from the officers' horses and the ambulance teams until we starved the horses almost to death. We would pick up corn that the horses would waste and wash it and parch it.

W. H. Harris of Farmersville also reported stealing corn from the horses during the last week of the war, which he called the hardest service he ever saw:

We had nothing to eat except corn, which we parched. We reached the state that it was common to see the men pick up corn around where the horses were fed, and after washing it off, somewhat, parched it and thought it was good.

Not only was food scarce, but cooking utensils also, as reported by **Martin Vanburen Gribble of Temple** from the battle of Perryville:[25]

The battle of Perryville was the only regular battle I was in. Was in some skirmishing at Cheat Mountain, Va.[26] and also in Tennessee. One afternoon before the battle of Perryville we stopped on a creek and drew three days rations of flour, and received orders to cook and be ready for march by five o'clock next morning. We had nothing to make dough in and nothing to cook with. As luck would have it we found that we were in a sugar orchard, and found some little sugar troughs. My mess got one and made the dough up in it. We made a little trough and got some sticks and rolled the dough around one end about a foot long, and held it over the fire until the outside was cooked. We would prepare many in this

---

24 Lookout Mountain, Tennessee, November 24, 1863.

25 Perryville (Chaplin Hills), Kentucky, October 8, 1862.

26 Cheat Mountain, western Virginia, September 11-13, 1861.

way, then would open the hot ashes and lay them in like roasting potatoes. We cooked three days rations in this way and started the next morning at the appointed time. This was all the bread we had for three weeks. We got some beef in the mountains and broiled it over the fire without any salt.

Corn remained the number one item of the Rebel diet, which caused another problem, mass disentary, but **John E. Logsdon of Gainesville** found another way to have his corn and eat it too:

The first three days of our stay at Cumberland Gap we had nothing to eat but parched corn. Two ears of corn each day to each man was all the rations issued. I was always very fond of coffee, and would parch my corn thoroughly brown, beat it up fine and make a cup of coffee three times a day. After drinking the coffee, I ate the grounds, thereby getting all the stimulant and nourishment there was in the corn.

W. S. McShan of Forestburg fought in Tennessee from Murfreesboro[27] to Perryville and at Chattanooga[28] and Lookout Mountain and underwent hardships "that no one can tell":

We got for rations a small pone of corn bread and a smaller piece of "Jerked" beef and three little cakes of bread as a full day's rations. It was no uncommon thing for us to eat it all at once, and do without the remainder of the day. We were only half clad and barefooted, but always went where we were ordered, faced death or anything else that was in the line of duty.

---

27 Murfreesboro (Stone's Mountain), Tennessee, December 31 to January 2, 1863.

28 Chattanooga, Tennessee, campaigns in October and November of 1863.

Afterglow

On the morning of April 9, 1865, Palm Sunday, Lee and Grant met to discuss the terms of surrender in the home of Wilmer McLean at Appomattox Court House. On the twelfth of April, a cloudy Wednesday, the final surrender took place and as the beaten Southern troops marched silently past the Federals, a Union general commented, "An awed stillness, and breath-holding, as if it were the passing of the dead." When the guns were finally silenced, the ragged Confederates headed for home, or at least they hoped there was a home to go back to. Some walked for hundreds of miles with empty sleeves, or hobbled on homemade crutches.

George Bruton Bragg of Gomez returned home to the surprise of his family:

When I left home for the war my father called me to him and laid his hand on my head and requested me, if I got the worst of it and ever came home to wear the same kind of clothes I went away in. I came home July 14, 1865. They thought I was a stranger, and asked me to come in. I asked him to come and look at these clothes and see if they would do, and he said, "Come in, you are welcome, my boy." I am prouder of that uniform today than any clothes I ever wore. I would describe them to you, but it would not look well in print. If they could have been admitted at a "Tacky Party" they would have taken the cake. I am proud of the clothes today, but like all the thoroughbred "Rebs" have buried the hatchet and accepted the inevitable, but still cherish the memory of the proud little flag and the tacky suit of clothes.

But not all of the "Rebs" were reconstructed. **M. A. Cooper of Breckinridge** wasn't in 1912 when he wrote:

General Bee[1] was commanding my brigade at the time he gave Gen. T. J. Jackson the name of "Stonewall." I was in the war four years and am still an unreconstructed rebel, and will answer the last "roll call" as one.

And unfortunately, not all the Rebs had to wait until the end of the war to go home. **Jas. Adams of Austin** was born in Ireland. It was a short war for Adams, who enlisted on April 19, 1861:

I was wounded at Malvern Hill,[2] Va. on July 11, 1862 in both legs. Had both legs amputated—one two inches below the knee joint and one four inches below the hip joint. Was discharged on July 16, on account of disabilities.

Archibald Gray Adams of Marshall, who dreamed of the battle of Shiloh[3] while in prison, was with General Joseph Johnston at the surrender in North Carolina:

Here these poor, worn-out, ragged, barefooted soldiers received the sum of $1.25 each for four years service and the dollar was a Mexican dollar. The twenty-five cents he was obliged to spend, but the dollar is handed down to his children and grandchildren, a silent history of the "men who wore the gray."

And after all those years, **Abraham Frisby of Trinity** remained a Rebel to the core:

Was never wounded or captured. I always out run the Yankees. I was a secessionist in 1861 and am still one.

---

1   Barnard Elliott Bee's family moved to Texas when he was a boy.

2   Malvern Hill, Virginia. Also Crew's Farm, Poindexter's Farm. July 1, 1862.

3   Shiloh, Tennessee. Also known as Pittsburg Landing. April 6-7, 1862.

Going home was not always a joyful thing. **George W. Duncan of San Angelo** found very little left:

I arrived home the 1st of April, 1865, with the remainder of Lee's disbanded men, and found everything on my mother's plantation destroyed. Every building gone and most of the fencing, not enough material of building left to build a respectable hencoop; the brick chimneys had been hauled off to their headquarters.

J. H. Conrson of Como reflected on those many who did not make it home:

My Capt. Reedy was in the Mexican war. He was a good drill officer, but very wicked. He was killed at Chickamauga.[4] I was three feet of him when he fell. The last word he spoke was "Oh, Lord!" I picked up his sword when it fell. Capt. Jones was my last Captain, and was a brave Christian man. He was a native of Georgia. My company was mustered in with about three hundred men, only thirty of us remained to tell the sad story.

Like a lot of the veterans, **Luke French of Pilot Point** was certain they would all meet again:

God bless them all, and may we all meet at the final Roll Call where there will be no sufferings and hardships of war.

And like **David Douglas of Van Alstyne,** most of them were so anxious to get home, they forgot to surrender and were financed by their commanding officer:

At the close of the war a few of us started home without being discharged, but some were recaptured. I made it through and have never surrendered. When the war was over and some few of us tried to make it home without surrendering, Gen. Wheeler[5] gave us four dollars each to help us along.

---

4   Chickamauga, Georgia, September 20, 1863.

It was not a particularly happy homecoming for **J. W. Leslie of McKinney**:

Near the close of the war we were ordered to Galveston, but before we reached there the war closed and we came home to find nothing but a naked farm. Everything had been taken away; horses, cattle and hogs. My dear old mother and a negro woman with two children was all that was there when I arrived. That dear old mother and negro woman spun and wove all the clothes and blankets that I had during the war.

William Howard of Brownfield came home and found his family had moved:

When I got to the old home I found that my old parents had "refugeed" to Texas, and I found them near Pilot Grove, Grayson County, July 15, 1865, just four years from the date of enlistment. Like a great many other boys, what I had left was on my back, and that was badly worn, but I went to work under "Carpetbag Rule," gritted my teeth and bore it.

William Lot Davidson of Richmond assisted in the capture of the Federals at San Antonio when the state seceded and expressed the feeling of most of the men for the Southern ladies:

While I believe I belonged to a brigade that suffered more, faced and fought greater odds, fought and won as many victories as any brigade in the Southern Army, still I do not claim that I was individually a great soldier; at the same time I have no apology to make to any man for my conduct during those four years of carnage, but to the Confederate woman I do apologize for, after seeing her sacrifices, her fortitude and suffering, I think I might have fought a little harder and suffered still more.

---

5   Joseph "Fightin' Joe" Wheeler.

George Everett Estes of Fort Worth left home in 1861 with a mission:

I started out in May, 1861, from home with the expressed intention of cleaning up all Yankeedom. I had been taught by demagogues and politicians to believe that I could whip a "cow pen full" of common Yankees. I behaved and acted under this delusion till Gen. Grant and his army met us at Fort Donelson.[6] *I soon found that the Yankees could shoot as far and as accurately as I could and from then until the end of the war I was fully of the opinion that the United States Army was fully prepared to give me all the fight I wanted.*

This change was reflected in his homecoming, after four years of war and prison:

I came home in May, 1865, not gay and scrappy as I started out, but a full-grown man, well versed in hardships, privations, dangers, and the art of war. I was as tame as an old mule, and all I wanted in this life was some old clothes and something to eat.

And he was not the only one who had changed and only wanted peace, as **D. W. Dodson of Texarkana** reported:

I served four years in the Confederate Army and was but a mere boy when I enlisted. I had the misfortune to lose three brothers at the battle of Manassas,[7] *Va. I reached home alive, but not sound. I was sick a long time after my arrival home.*

The wordy **Louis Spencer Flatau of St. Louis** summed up his memoirs with:

---

6   Fort Donelson, Tennessee campaign, February 12 through 16, 1862.

7   Battles took place at Manassas, Virginia, on July 21, 1861, and
     August 29-30, 1862.

The battle of Franklin[8] seemed to have been intended to be as it was, and, I believe that the great God of all war, and the Maker of all men received the souls of those who fell as they took their flight that dark, cold night from the bloody field into Heaven, where they still remain waiting and watching for those of the same kind to come and be with them forever more.

Another unrepentant Confederate was **William Hugh Graham of Athens** who wrote, after more than forty years of reflection:

We were ordered back to Greensboro, N.C., and formed into as compact a body as was possible, and here received our first official notice that Gen. Lee had surrendered. That was the most solemn occasion of the whole war, and it seemed so to others. Gen. Johnston and his aide rode into the center and he had his orderly read the dispatches from Lee to himself. I never saw as still an army in all my life. Each was trying to catch every word. After the reading was over, Gen. Johnston tried to make a talk to his men, but broke down, and quit with saying but little. My recollection is that his last words were; "Go home, boys, and make as good citizens as you have soldiers." It was a sad day with us. Not that we were bloodthirsty, but we did not know what the result would be. We felt that our cause was just, and that we had a right to defend our rights—and I believe so yet. I am one of those who believe that the Sons and Daughters of the Confederacy are born of heroic blood, and that the historic fields and incidents of that brave struggle are in good hands.

J. L. Greer of McKinney continued to agonize over the defeat of the South:

---

8   Franklin, Tennessee, November 30, 1864.

Our humiliation in defeat (not defeat, but failure) has caused more than mental pain, and is harder to bear, than all the exposure, hunger and wounds during the war. It rankles me in my heart still, and I am not reconstructed yet. I want this on my tombstone; "Here lies a Confederate soldier."

And **R. T. Young of Sulphur Springs** said:

I have never had reason to change my views concerning the war, and have done what I could to keep alive the fires of patriotism which we kindled in the early '60s.

James T. Hall of Farmhill, Louisiana echoed the distress of the beaten Confederate:

I do not remember having unsaddled my horse nor did I lay down to sleep during the entire retreat, sleeping mostly on my horse. At last came that fatal day when it seemed impossible to resist longer. Grant, through Gen. Custer, had demanded a surrender. Gen. Grant having sent his staff officers to escort Gen. Lee to his headquarters for consultation as to the surrender. Gen. Lee dressed in his best suit and mounted on his old gray charger looking every inch a soldier, passed through our lines, cheered by loving soldiers, while tears rolled down their sun-burnt cheeks, never did he look more noble and grand than he did on that sad day, and never was a General more beloved and honored by his men than Gen. Robert E. Lee. Thus ended, on the field of Appomattox, the long and desperate struggle for our homes and what we deemed our rights.

A. J. King of Wolfe City was seventeen years old when he joined up, and found himself a long way from home when it was over:

Was never captured until Gen. Lee surrendered at Appomattox on April 9, 1865, where I was turned loose 800 miles from home to get there as best I could. In the absence of any other kind of transportation, I walked.

Richard Kerby of Farmersville found his wife gone but his children in good hands, even if they didn't know who he was:

On my way home I passed by where my mother-in-law lived. My wife had died. I saw some children playing in the woodpile. I recognized them as my own, and asked them to go in the house and see if they would give me something to eat. When the girl came back I asked her if she knew me and she said "No." I then told her I was her father. She went back into the house and told her grandmother that that old ragged soldier out there said he was her papa. Mrs. Hughes came to see, and sure enough it was true. We had a good meeting.

Madison D. Harrell of South Bend was not released from prison in Chicago until some time after the surrender, which made his homecoming more special:

My home was about 100 miles southeast of Memphis, and I had to walk part of the way. Had not heard from home in a long time. When passing the homes we could see someone looking for their loved ones, and finally I came in sight of my home, and who do you think I saw? It was my dear old mother at the door looking for her boy. Oh, how she ran to meet me. At home again, and best of all, at home to stay.

For many who served the war never ended, as in the case of **Minyard H. Harris of Kirvin** who had the unpleasant and unpopular task of arresting deserters and returning them to their commands:

After the war, when the Federals had control of the country, I was reported as having run down white men with bloodhounds in order to send them back to the army; so I was in constant danger of being caught and shot or hanged; but I only escaped by being absent when wanted.

Brothers **William Walter Mabry** and **J. J. Mabry of Llano** served in different units during the war but came home together, much to the delight of family and pets. J. J. wrote the memories, as William had passed away when the survey was taken:

At the break-up of Debray's and Wood's regiment we were at Houston to protect the property of citizens as much as possible. On the 18th day of April, 1865, after shaking hands and bidding adieu to the officers and men, by accident and in the confusion of disbanding, these two brothers met and wended their way homeward to San Saba, Tx. Hallowed memory! As these two soldiers of the lost cause rode up to the old home, father and mother came to meet them, praising God; sisters came joyously to join the happy company and express their feelings, and the two old family watchdogs had the times of their lives.

David Oliver Newton of Hico admits in his remembrance that he got home a little ahead of the other Confederate soldiers:

We retreated and crossed the Tennessee River at Murel Shoals, some twenty miles above Florence, Ala., where we crossed on our advance to Nashville. We found lodgement at Columbus, Miss., for a few days, and then started to join Lee in Virginia. I took a kind of French furlough as we passed through Montgomery, Ala., to go by home to see what had become of my old parents, and never reached my company again. The large part of them were captured at Salisbury, N.C. The remainder, learning that Lee had surrendered, made their way back home. I was in Athens, Ga., when the news first reached me. I returned to my father's home and went to repairing the farm which Sherman's men had almost destroyed. I was minus three brothers—Lewis H. Newton, killed at Resaca, Ga.; William A. Newton, died of camp fever in East Tennessee; and Clark Newton, died in Savannah, Ga. All belonged to the Confederate army.

But **J. W. Ozier of Amarillo** stayed until the bitter end:

I was there and saw the old flag furled, the guns grounded and have my parole.... unreconstructed.

W. R. McBee of Austin also felt no regrets for his service in the Confederate army:

Was wounded in the head June 1, 1864 at Raccoon Ford[9] and severely wounded at Mannassas and knocked down at Chickamauga.[10] Was captured March 7th at Appomattox Court House. I went to the army from a sense of duty, not that I wanted military honors, but am just as much a Confederate now as I was then.

William F. McKee of Grand Saline who was over forty years old when he enlisted in the Confederate army found a grand welcome when he came home:

Just before the close of the war my regiment was ordered to report to E. Kirby Smith at Shreveport, La. Here we were dismounted and our horses taken from us. Of course, we were paid for them in Confederate money which was well nigh worthless. (I gave a twenty dollar bill for a black plug of tobacco.) In a few days we were ordered to Houston, Texas. This was only a short time before the surrender. So we took the line of march for Houston and owing to the fact that I had sustained a fracture of the bones in my ankle when a boy and not being accustomed to walking, my ankle gave out on the second day and was so swollen and sore that it was impossible for me to keep up. The captain told me to drop out

---

9   Raccoon Ford, Alabama, skirmish on October 30, 1864.

10   Chickamauga, Georgia, September 20, 1863.

and he would send the ambulance back for me. I spread my blanket on the ground and while lying there an old citizen came along in a one horse cart and took me to a hospital at Old Kechi, La. I remained there for two weeks and got so that I could walk a little when news came that Lee had surrendered to Grant and that Kirby Smith of the Trans-Mississippi Department, had disbanded his troops and they were making their way home. Fortunately some calvarymen came along who had belonged to my brigade, eight of them, and one man named Black was leading a horse. I still had my revolvers and traded one of them for an old saddle, mounted Black's horse and rode within fifty miles of home where I borrowed a horse to ride the remainder of the way. Imagine my feeling when I got within sight of home. Here I met a good old mother and kind sister who had made their own living most of the time since I had been gone, as my father had died early in 1863. My mother was one of the "Old Timers" and knew how to spin and weave and soon had her boy clothed in a nice suit. She had two other sons in the Confederate Army who never returned, one being killed at Corinth,[11] Miss., and the other at New Iberia,[12] La.

McKee added a final touch of sadness and a promise of hope to his memories:

I am totally deaf and a lonely Old Reb. Still there is a warm place in my heart for the old "Vets," and expect to soon answer the last roll call.

---

11   Corinth, Mississippi, October 3, 1862.

12   Confederate salt works were destroyed April 18, 1863.

After participating in four of the most horrible battles of the war, Fredericksburg,[13] Chancellorsville,[14] the Wilderness,[15] and Gettysburg,[16] **Henry A. Morehead of McGregor** closed out the war in Montgomery, Alabama, working in a government shoe shop. But soon the war was over and he headed home:

As soon as we got our paroles we wended our way homeward. The railroads being torn up we were four days getting back to Montgomery, Ala., where we found the city overrun with negro troops. Here we lay and put up with negro insolence for six days before we could get transportation. We dared not open our mouths for fear of a riot, so decided to say nothing and keep out of the way as much as possible. We all had something of value which we would need when we would get home. We could not walk and carry them, so made the best of it. Amongst other things I had bought two yards of calico to make my wife a bonnet, for which I had paid $13, and was considered lucky to get it at all. After much worry and trouble I reached my home and loved ones on May 14, 1865, but not so gay and sprightly as when I went away. Just what to do I did not know. It was too late to make a crop, and not a dollar except "Confed," not a bushel of corn, nor a pound of meat; nothing but a wife and child. So you see I was in the middle of a bad fix. I had over $50,000 in Confederate money, but as it was worth nothing, I was advised to give it to my children to play with, but I said, "No; I will keep it to show to my grandchildren"; and I have the money yet, and the grandchildren to show it to.

---

13   Fredericksburg, Virginia, December 13, 1862.

14   Chancellorsville, Virginia, May 1-4, 1863.

15   Battle of the Wilderness, Virginia, May 5-7, 1864.

16   Gettysburg, Pennsylvania, July 1-3, 1863.

Thomas Reed Murray of McKinney had children to come home to, but alas, he had been gone too long:

But there were two years that I did not even hear from home, and when I finally reached it my babies had forgotten me.

But like so many of the veterans, Murray remained true to the cause:

The sons of today look back on their four years' college course as the brightest and best years of their lives, and I, despite the horrors of war, found the same inspiring comradeship in my four years' course. But time has not graduated me into an ex-Confederate yet; I am only an ex-soldier.

Like most of the veterans, **David H. Williams of McGregor** came home to almost nothing after closing out the war at Rock Island[17] prison, but was thankful for what was left:

I reached home on the night of June 30th and there was the happiest time of my life. Here were my wife and six children all well, though there was not a bushel of corn on the place, and but little in the smokehouse.

Not much was left for **S. W. Thompson of Anson** to come home to, either:

Got home and found everything gone. Not a good horse in the country except those brought for the army. But we went to work to build up the waste places, and strange to say, in three years you could not tell that we had been to war except now and then an empty sleeve or a one-legged man. The men who were great in war have proved themselves the yoemen of the South in peace.

---

17 Rock Island prison was on the Mississippi between Rock Island, Illinois, and Davenport, Iowa.

Jno. C. West of Waco took a companion home with him, and they enjoyed the good life after the war together:

I started for Waco, Texas. I remember that my pony, only about thirteen hands high, was put to his mettle and reached Waco late in the evening of Arpil 20th, 1864. I kept him as a souvenir until after the war closed, and had many glorious days with him in the woods, where deer and wild turkey were in abundance. He became a family pet, and with hounds, horn, and guns, his memory is interwoven with some of the happiest associations of my life. He bore the classical and euphonious name of "Button."

And many years after the guns were silenced, **Johnathan (Jot) Woodall of Farmersville** renewed an old friendship:

The thing which made the most impression on me was about my comrade who was shot in front of Petersburg.[18] *I took him on my back and carried him to the hospital to die. I thought he was bleeding to death. I never saw nor heard of him again till the reunion in Dallas, Texas, when it seemed as if he had risen from the dead. If no one else had a reunion in Dallas, we did.*

John H. Wood of Graham reflected on the war years, the time of recovery, and never forgot that dear old song:

We went through sufferings and privations that the present generation can not realize. We were overpowered and had to lay down our arms, and for awhile we were under carpet bag rule and every disadvantage. From the ashes of homes destroyed have sprung many of the most beautiful homes on the American continent. All over our dear Southland stand hundreds of cities with their dense populations and with our grand institutions of learning. I love my dear old Dixie

---

18 Petersburg campaign from August 21 to October 27, 1864.

Land and am always ready to applaud when I hear that grand old tune, "Dixie."

W. J. Graham of McGregor hoped to pass on the Confederate spirit to his children:

Altogether I was fortunate to get out alive though I am still disabled from wounds in the body. When Lee surrendered that settled the war, though the principles for which I fought still burn as bright and strong as in 1861. I am proud I was a Confederate soldier and never shirked a duty, and have no apologies to make the United States government for my soldier life and I want my children to forever defend the principles for which we fought four long years.

But **John T. Poe of Longview,** after four years of fighting and many more of reflection, found himself in agreement with Sam Houston, who had opposed Texas entering the war:

I heard Sam Houston make a speech during the days just before secession, in which he said: "Bring on the war, gentlemen, as you now propose to do, and whether you whip in the fight or not you'll meet a taxgatherer at every street corner." How true! Gen. Houston urged us to remain in the Union and fight for our rights under the Stars and Stripes. I think he was right.

The High and the Mighty

One of the driving forces that kept the Confederate soldier in the field in spite of the hardships, suffering, and death was the unshakable belief that their cause was just and they were fighting to protect homes and families from the Yankee hordes. Another was their devotion and confidence in their leaders. With generals such as Lee, Jackson, and Gordon, it became a religious crusade to many. Their almost adoration of these leaders stayed with them until Appomattox and lingered yet in 1912.

Chas. W. Geers of Pilot Point had a very high opinion of his commanding officer:

A little after 2 o'clock Gen. Johnston[1] was killed. He had exposed himself unnecessarily. He had been in the front of the Fifth from its beginning, and his clothes had been riddle with minie balls. But he heeded it not. In the enthusiasm of the battle he was with his men cheering them to deeds of valor. He was shot in the leg. An artery was severed. He was at the time leading Col. Statham's magnificent brigade. He gave no heed to the wound, but continued the charge, bareheaded, with his hand elevated, riding a large gray horse. The charge was successful. He grew weak and reeled in his saddle. His staff officers came to his assistance, but they could do him no good. They carried him to a ravine where he died in a few minutes. He was one of God's noblemen. His

---

1   General Albert Sidney Johnston.

memory will ever be cherished. Had he lived another day Grant and Buell would have been wiped from the earth.

At the battle of the Wilderness,[2] Robert E. Lee's men would not let him lead them in battle, according to **James T. Hall of Farmhill, Louisiana:**

We went into the battle not having time to form line, so desperate was the battle raging. It was here that I saw our grand old Chieftain as he sat on his grey horse and as we were passing I saw the tears streaming down his cheeks, saying forward boys I will lead you, the shout went up, "never"—and while an officer held his horse by the bits, we rushed into the battle and soon turned the tide and Lee's army was saved.

Burton Rieves Conerly of Marshall reported a similar incident at Spotsylvania:[3]

We soon left the narrow road and crossed a freshly plowed field, made soft by the recent rain, and soon came to harder ground and crossed at right angles the "Old Stonewall" brigade lying on the ground. The writer heard one of them say: "Boys, you are going to catch h__ today." Gen. R. E. Lee had accompanied Gen Harris to this point, when the men begged him to go no farther, and the cry; "Gen. Lee to the rear!" was heard all along the line.

It seems that none of the Confederates who were present when Brig. Gen. Felix Kirk Zollicoffer was killed at Mills Springs could forget him or the day, as testified by **G. W. Speck of Brownwood:**

I served twelve months in the Twenty-Fifth Tennessee Infantry and was in the battle of Fishing Creek[4] where

---

2   Battle of the Wilderness, May 5 to 7, 1864.

3   Spotsylvania Court House campaign, May 7 through 19, 1864.

Zollicoffer was killed. This was the spring of 1862. He was killed through mistake. The enemy surrendered but before we had a chance to take charge of them they received reinforcements and Zollicoffer rode in front of them and was shot from his horse. After that we fell back to where we had breastworks.

Like Zollicoffer, every man remembered the time when Stonewall Jackson was killed, but **Alf. H. H. Tolar of Houston** had special and painful memories:

Stonewall Jackson[5] was wounded at Chancellorsville[6] in front of my company and regiment. He and staff and A. P. Hill and staff rode down the plank road to look out the position of enemy. We were waiting for orders for a night charge. Gen. Jackson and his party left the road to avoid a battery which had been trained upon them, and were coming in front of us and we, thinking it was a calvary charge, were ordered by Col. Pardue, to commence firing, which we kept up till informed by Capt. Morrison, an Aide de Camp of Jackson. He had ridden into our lines under heavy fire and gave us the first intimation that we were firing into Gen. Jackson's staff.

Some historians have reported that doctors think Jackson might have lived had not his stretcher bearers been shot, causing them to drop the general, reopening his wounds. **John Overton Casler of Oklahoma City** was there:

It was sometime during the shelling that Gen. Jackson was wounded. That night, it seems, Gen. Jackson and his staff had gone in front of our line of skirmishers to

---

4   Mill Springs, Kentucky. The battle took place on January 19, 1862, not in the spring.

5   His arm amputated, Jackson lived for eight days after the incident.

6   Chancellorsville, Virginia, May 1-4, 1863.

reconnoiter, in order to throw his corps between the enemy and the river, when he met their line of skirmishers advancing. He wheeled at once and came back rapidly. Our line mistaking him and his staff for the enemy, fired a volley into them with fatal effect, killing several of them and wounding others. Gen Jackson was shot through the right hand and received two balls through the left arm. He had to lie there during the shelling, and nearly bled to death before his wounds were staunched. They finally got him on a stretcher and started to the rear, when some of the bearers were cut down and he fell heavily to the ground, opening the wounds afresh. They finally got him to the ambulance, and he was taken to the field hospital, where Dr. Hunter McGuire amputated his left arm near the shoulder.

Another officer held in high esteem by the men was Albert Sidney Johnston, who was killed at Shiloh,[7] and **Charles W. Stone of Hondo** was certain it made a difference in the outcome of the war:

I have always thought that the bullet which hit Albert Sidney Johnston at Shiloh was the one which saved Grant's Army and sealed the fate of the Southern cause.

W. M. Willis of Rosenberg even had a kind word for perhaps the most maligned officer in the Southern army:

I wish to say a word for Gen. Winder,[8] our commander at Andersonville, who was blamed for what he could not help. He did the best he could under the circumstances.

---

7   Shiloh, also known as Pittsburgh Landing, April 6-7, 1862.

8   John Henry Winder was in charge of Andersonville prison in Georgia, the most renowned of Southern prisons. He died in 1865 of strain and fatigue.

Aron Wilburn of Honey Grove reported on at least one officer who cared about his men enough to do something about it:

After we got through the Cumberland Gap we met the army coming back to Knoxville, Tenn. The weather being very cold and a big snow on the ground we suffered greatly. I saw men marching in the ranks, barefooted, who at home were worth $20,000. Their feet were bleeding and they were nearly destitute of clothing. When we got to Knoxville the officers could draw their pay but the privates could not. Lieut. B. M. Orton of our company went around over the country and bought all the goods he could find. Some of the people cut it out of the looms and sold it to him. He brought it to the camps and had it made into clothes for our company. A better man never lived, at least when it come to dividing with his comrades, and today he would give the last cent he had to relieve an old Confederate soldier.

But according to **D. N. Yeary of Pilot Point**, not all the officers were held in such high esteem, even by their peers:

About the middle of September we were ordered to Cumberland Gap to hold and guard that place. We were dismounted and put under the command of Col. Frazier and I am sorry to say we were surrendered without a proper effort at resistance. This was one of the saddest things of the war. We could have held the Gap against almost any kind of odds. Our Captain jumped on Col. Frazier and would have given him a good thrashing but the Yankee officers pulled him off. It was indeed a sad thing to see nearly 2,000 brave boys in gray lay down their arms without a fight and be marched off to prison.

Solomon Thomas Blessing of Fort Worth recalls the memorable charge at the battle of the Wilderness:[9]

I fell behind to do some visiting and did not catch up with the command till they had made the memorable charge at the Wilderness, where Gen. Lee, seeing them coming, asked who they were, and on being told that it was Hood's Texas Brigade, said; "I have confidence in them," and started to lead them but was prevented by the boys crying, "Go back, Daddy, we will go without you."

But to **Louis Spencer Flatau of St. Louis,** none of the Confederate generals, or for that matter, leaders of all time, compared to the Texan who led him into battle. To prove his point, he quoted none other than Jefferson Davis:

I don't think that I digress if I call your attention to some of the facts in regard to this wonderful patriot. No one can dispute the greatness and patriotism of our Generals in the Confederate Army. You have heard the names of Lee, Johnston, Beauregard and Hardee. 'Lustrious Stonewall Jackson and other sung and spoken throughout this country, but I want to give you the highest authority of the Confederacy that my ideas of his greatness are true. To do that, I want to remind you of a man who was the greatest and grandest statesman, hero and citizen the world ever knew. Napoleon wasn't a circumstance, the Duke of Welling was nowhere, and Abraham Lincoln couldn't hold a candle to him. All sink into insignificance, in my estimation, compared to this man.

Flatau goes on to list the battles his hero fought in and the hardships endured before he finally names him in words spoken by Davis:

I am going to send you back to Tennessee. I can't promise you much breadstuff, I can't promise you much comfort; you will undergo many, many privations and suffering, no

---

9   Battle of the Wilderness in Virginia, May 5-7, 1864.

doubt, but there is one thing I will promise you—a man to lead you to victory, or even to defeat, the grandest, the most patriotic officer and soldier that ever drew a sword from its Sheath, Gen. John B. Hood of Texas.

Sterling Price of Missouri was another officer held in high esteem by his men, as recorded by **J. F. Smith of Morgan**:

Gen. Price was always as kind and thoughtful of us as possible. He called us his "boys" and we called him "Pap." Frequently he would give his horse to some weary soldier and he would walk in the ranks.

James Knox Polk Yeary of McGregor spoke highly of Gen. Richard Montgomery Gano:[10]

Late in the spring the gallant Gen R. M. Gano was put in command, and his tactics were a surprise to the Federals. The second day after he assumed command he called for volunteers to make a raid, and in a talk told us that he did not want any man who was afraid of Yankee powder and bullets. After the raid he had no trouble to get his men to follow him, and he never asked them to go where he would not go himself.

General Gano, born in Kentucky, moved to Texas in 1859 and after the war, returned to serve as a Protestant clergyman. He was active in the United Confederate Veterans until his death in Dallas on March 27, 1913.

And some officers, in spite of victory in the field, got very little respect, as reported by **W. H. Hudson of Edna**:

Gen. Dick Taylor, who was in command, being reinforced by Price's[11] Corps from Missouri, met the enemy near Mansfield,[12] La. Taylor had orders from Kirby Smith to fall

---

10   Richard Montgomery Gano of Kentucky.

11   Sterling "Pap" Price of Missouri.

12   Mansfield (Pleasant Grove), Louisiana, April 8, 1864.

*back to Shreveport, but knowing the condition of Bank's[13]
army, one corps being one day's travel behind the other, he
formed line of battle and engaged Banks at Mansfield, La.
Here we completely routed them, capturing about 2,800 prisoners and about seventy-five six-mile wagons, loaded with
supplies and thirty pieces of artillery.*

*The next day Kirby Smith[14] arrived and placed Gen.
Dick Taylor under arrest for giving battle. Taylor remarked
that it was the first time in the history of the world that a
General was placed under arrest for whipping the enemy.*

The Confederate soldiers looked up to their own leaders but
had very little respect for the generals in blue. And according
to **Leland Kennedy Jackson of Sulphur Springs**, his opinion of one Federal officer lessened long after the war was
over:

*Gen. Grant, while at Holly Springs,[15] occupied as head-
quarters the fine residence of the wealthy citizen, Will Henry
Cox. Mrs. Grant remained there, and, as she thought, took up
winter quarters with entire security. When she left, true to
Yankee cupidity, Mrs. Cox's fine collection of silvered-plate
disappeared also. One very fine silver vase marked with family name: "Permelia," was also missing. Afterwards, when
Mrs. Grant occupied the White House, strange as it may
seem, that same vase was amoungst the table decorations of
the President's home. A local paper at Holly Springs men-
tioned the matter at the time, and it was identified by parties
who knew it.*

---

13 Union General Nathaniel Prentiss Banks.

14 Edmund Kirby Smith of Florida.

15 Holly Springs, Mississippi, raid on December 20, 1862.

A Funny Thing Happened on the Way to War

Not all the boys in gray took the war seriously, and there were lighter moments, even in the thick of battle, in the camp, or even in prison. Perhaps some of the humor was to mask the fear inside, but there were some who just believed in having fun wherever they were and no matter what they were doing. There were also the practical jokers.

After writing of the horrors of war at Gettysburg,[1] **J. F. Lewis of Austin** reported:

In those days we were young and full of life, and did not take things seriously, but always had something in the way of fun, as well as suffering and sorrow. On one occasion in the spring we played a joke on a new Corporal. There were twenty-two posts around our command, and we agreed to keep him on the run all night. First guard called out; "Corporal of the guard, 1." It was his duty to answer such calls and relieve the sentinel for a short time. About the time he would get back to guard quarters he was called to another post, and in this way he was kept on the run till just before dawn. Then "Corporal of the post, 22," was called out, and when he got there he was sure mad, and said, "What in the Jim Bob do you want?" "Well, Corporal, here is a gentleman who wants to pass in." "Where is he?" The guard pointed to a toad and said: "There he is."

---

1   Gettysburg, Pennsylvania, July 1 through 3, 1863.

According to **R. W. Hurdle of Winnsboro**, there were even lighter moments in the heat of battle:

Some one stated that it was the Sixth Mississippi Regiment that was so fearfully slaughtered in charging Prentiss[2] at the point called the Hornet's nest at Shiloh.[3] It was the Sixth Tennessee. They had been held in reserve all morning, but at the moment they were hurled into the jaws of death. All was silent in the front until our ranks were near. Then came an incessant hail of lead and iron until our line was strewn with the dying and wounded. The remainder had to lie down for protection. In a few minutes a Mississippi Regiment dashed up, and as they passed over our line, called out: "Get out of the way, Tennessee, and let Mississippi in." They passed on for a short distance and returned on double quick, and as they passed a Tennessee fellow said: "Get out of the way, Tennessee, and let Mississippi out."

Johnson Busbee Harris of Karnes City found that even orders could be misconstrued:

While stationed here the Yankees came to Independence, about ten miles from us. Col. Edmonson ordered me to take five men and picket the cross roads, midway between the two places. It was a glorious ride over a smooth road. When we reached the place designated, we received a sharp order to halt. My first command to my men was to get out of the road, but our conception of the command differed somewhat. Where I meant for them to go was to the sides of the road, to avoid all being shot at once. Their idea was to reach the farthest end of it, in the quickest possible time. For all we know, two of them have not reached it yet.

---

2   Benjamin Mayberry Prentiss.

3   Shiloh (Pittsburg Landing), Tennessee, April 6 and 7, 1862.

H. H. Hoyley of Robert Lee reported another excellent runner at Harrisburg:[4]

At Harrisburg they took the starch out of us. We had one man who ran off from there, and if he has ever stopped I have never heard of it. He ran ninety miles the first day and the last we heard of him he was still going at a lively gait.

And **Thomas Crawford Hoy of Swenson** was honest enough to tell why he was never captured:

I was never captured, but sometimes I out ran them.

Tom Hill of Wolfe City, whose memoirs were written by this comrade, **H. M. Harrison,** also **of Wolfe City,** gives an account of the battle of Ocean Pond,[5] and a glimpse at the Confederate soldiers' determination, and temper:

At Ocean Pond, a Yankee armed with a repeating rifle and behind a tree, kept shooting at him. Tom got tired of this, so he left the ranks and went straight towards the Yankee, who continued to fire, missing him every shot. Tom caught him in the collar and led him back through our lines, then took his place in the ranks coolly as if nothing had happened. This fight at Ocean Pond was one of the hardest of the war, for the Yankees out-numbered us three to one. At Fort Harrison[6] he was on the litter corps. A fellow by the name of Thurmond was knocked down by a ball and lay as if dead. Tom remarked that the "niggers" should not have him, so he crawled on his hands and knees to where the fellow lay, and said to him, "Can't you crawl?" Thurmond replied that he could, and began crawling towards our line, Tom crawling behind to shield him. When they got near our lines

---

4   Harrisburg, Mississippi, July 14 and 15, 1864.

5   Ocean Pond, Florida, February 20, 1864.

6   Fort Harrison (Chaffin's Farm), Virginia, September 29 and 30, 1864.

Thurmond rose and ran, beating Tom to the lines. Tom was the maddest man ever saw.

G. B. Ford of Bangs served in Jackson's Corps:

Just before the battles of Cross Keys,[7] *Seigle*[8] *tried to get in Jackson's rear and as the Yankees were marching by Gen. Lewis' home they were singing "Shackson in a Shug, Boys, Shackson in a shug." (They were Dutch) A few days later they came back, minus hat and gun when the young ladies hailed; "Hey, thought Shackson was in a shug." "Och! de stopper flew out."*

And at Gaine's Mill Bangs reported another incident:

The day after the battle of Gaine's Mill[9] *Jackson succeeded in taking the York River railroad, cutting off several of McClellan's trains. The enemy, finding they could not get them out, put a lighted fuse to an ordinance train and sent it down amongst us. The rush and the roar sounded like a cavalry charge. We were lying on the roadside resting when Gen. Ewell*[10] *came dashing down the line, "Attention!" We soon found out it was no cavalry charge. The car exploded doing no harm. An Irishman in our regiment looked wildly about and said: "Be Jasus! You had as well kill a man as to skeer him to death."*

Chas. W. Geers of Pilot Point kept his sense of humor, even in a tight situation:

At Duck Creek,[11] *Tenn., I was walking along a fence when a man rose and halted me. I thought it was our picket line,*

---

7   Cross Keys, Virginia, June 8, 1862.

8   German born Franz Sigel.

9   Gaines Mill, Virginia, June 27, 1863.

10   General Richard Stoddert Ewell, known by his men as "Old Bald Head."

and I answered that I was a friend of the South, when he told me I would go the other way. They took me to Gen. Wilson's[12] headquarters. I had on a blue overcoat. Gen. Wilson pointed to a seat. I gave him my name, state, and command. The General wanted to know why I had on a blue overcoat, and I told him it was to keep the rain off.

At Murfreesboro, **Charles Thomas Landrum of Fort Worth** thought he was a goner:

I had a very large canteen, and before the battle I had filled it with water. There were several piles of thick red flannel between the tin and the leather. Well, the Yankees shot a hole clear through my canteen and the ball pulled a fragment of red cloth through it. I could feel the trickling of the water down my leg and thought it was blood and saw the red string waving around and it looked like blood and I was sure that half of my hip had been shot away.

(Later he was really injured by a shell hitting his hip.)

The **Massey brothers of Marshall** fought in the same unit but were somewhat different, as **J. S. Jack Massey** reported:

Was detailed to spy out the enemy's position. My brother was along on account of his bravery, and I because I had a good horse.

Thomas Reed Murray of McKinney found some humor even in the deprivations of war:

On the raid in Missouri[13] I was often detailed as cook or litter bearer. I was known in camp and prison as "Polly," so I

---

11 Duck River, Tennessee. A number of events took place on this stream, but no major battle.

12 James Harrison Wilson died February 23, 1925, one of the last surviving Union generals.

13 General Sterling "Pap" Price's raid in the fall of 1864.

have to leave the sufferings, starvation, and the cruel usages of war for my more favored comrades to tell, as detailed workers were fed and clothed, though not always fitted. I remember one cold morning several of us on detailed duty were ordered to report and get some shoes. Barefooted we went, our names were called and a pair of shoes thrown at us. A comrade wore a No. 4; his name was Tom Brown, and he got a No. 12. I can see him yet, standing there in camp, his toes just reaching the eye seams of those huge shoes.

Even during times of hardships, boys will be boys, as **Robert McGuire of McCaulley** reported. Unlike most of the veterans, McGuire said he never had a day without something to eat and was at all times reasonably clad. All needed warm clothing in Georgia during the winter of 1864:

Here we had one of Georgia's biggest snow storms and had a snow ball battle between Strahl's[14] Tennessee Brigade and Jackson's[15] Georgia Brigade. After Jackson's men were run into camp they called on the General for a speech. He declined saying: "I am not competent to make you a speech, but hope when we meet the enemy you will be as successful in routing them as you have been in routing my men with snowballs."

But another officer learned the hard way not to try and stop the soldiers' "horseplay," as reported by **W. A. Nabours of Cameron**:

After our regimental reorganization we were quartered at Camp Bragg, near Richmond, and were required to drill in squads for several hours each day. One day while drilling

---

14   General Otho French Strahl was killed at the battle of Franklin, Tennessee.

15   General Henry Rootes Jackson.

Lieut. Sam Streetman halted the squad under the shade of a pine tree to rest. Here Lieutenant Streetman and one of the men got into a wrestle, and while thus engaged the Major, who had just been appointed and who was a foreigner by the name of Von Biberstein, or some other outlandish name, rode up and said: "Lieutenant, have you, as an officer, no more respect for yourself than to the equalizing yourself with a private soldier?" Lieut. Streetman's reply was not in the Sunday school lessons of those days. He also told the Major that any private soldier in his (Streetman's) company was as good, if not better, than he (the Major); and the night following the Major's horse's mane and tail were sheared close. In fact, the horse's tail was as sleek as an opossum's. We never heard from the Major after this.

F. M. Martin of Oglesby saw some hand-to-hand combat that became a finger-in-mouth fight:

An incident of the Truine[16] fight was the capture of two of our men, Capt. Conner and Joe McBride. They ran to a fence, but as it was wet from rain they couldn't get over it before the Yankee cavalry ran up and demanded surrender. Joe McBride turned on the Major with his gun; the Major had his sword, and they clinched. Joe came near biting the Major's finger off. It was hard to keep the soldiers from killing Joe. They took him to Gen. Osterhaus[17] and told him that here was the man who bit the Major's finger off, and asked what must be done with him. Gen. Osterhaus looked the prisoner over from head to foot and, turning to the guard, said: "I want you to accord him every respect due a prisoner, and I want every one of you to fight just like he did."

16 Truine, Tennessee, skirmishes took place here from 1862 through 1865.

17 German born Peter Joseph Osterhaus.

John W. Roberts of Vernon tells of one friend who had a premonition of death, and another who had a reason to risk death or capture:

At Brandy Station,[18] *Polk Preston, a comrade, bade farewell to his chums, saying he was going to be killed that day. He was ridiculed as there was no enemy near, but he was dead by noon. We had a hard fought battle and it took the entire day to drive the enemy back across the Rappahanock. Another chum, Clarence Payne, had a Yankee sweetheart who invited him to take tea with her on a certain night, and he asked me what he should do about it. I told him not to go without two good men. He hid the men near the house and walked into the parlor. Miss Ann Goodheart (the girl's name) met him very cordially and introduced him to a Yankee Lieutenant, and two other soldiers. Payne enjoyed the repast and occasion very much but soon after the latter was over the Yankee Lieutenant told him he was very sorry, but that he would have to arrest him and take him to Washington. They chatted a while longer, and Payne gave the signal, and his two Confederates rushed into the parlor, when Payne said, "I am very sorry, Lieutenant, but I will have to take you all to Richmond," which he did.*

J. M. Slayden of Sterrett gave an illustration of how dangerous it was to get a furlough:

We fought every day while we were in Tennessee. On the retreat from Nashville we formed line of battle, and as one of the boys was riding off the field his finger was shot off. He held up his hand and said: "Boys, this is good for ninety days' furlough." He got his furlough, all right, and went to

---

18 Brandy Station, Virginia, battle here on June 9, 1863. Skirmishes
    throughout war.

Kentucky, and the Yanks caught him and they thought so much of him that they kept him until the war closed.

A colorful incident was recorded by **Dr. Frank Rainey of Dallas** at the battle of Mansfield:

Then Gen. Taylor turned on his pursuers and completely routed them, capturing over 250 wagons loaded with provisions of all kinds, together with about 2,500 prisoners, amongst them was a regiment of New York Zouaves all dressed in red flannel trousers, looking somewhat like the ladies bloomers of later times. They wore dainty red caps with tassels and made a sight for the Texans to look at, and when they were marching by and were halted, the Texas troops pretended to get mad, swore because they had been compelled to fight women. Some of them threw down their guns and declared that if they were to fight any more women they would go home. The Zouaves thought the Texans were in earnest, and protested loudly that they were not women.

And **J. M. Polk of Austin** found that even a general could have a sense of humor:

We were all ignorant then about discipline in the army and thought that we had a right to know as much as the officers. But we soon found out differently. Gen. Whiting was an old army officer, and a good one, and he said to Gen. Hood, that he had no doubt but what those Texas men would make good soldiers, "but you will have a hard time getting them down to army regulations." Gen. Jackson was a good hand to execute and keep his own counsel, and about the first thing that he did was to give us to understand that we must know nothing but obey orders and if any citizen, on the march should ask you where you are going, tell them that you "don't know." The next day he came along and noticed one of our men leave ranks for a cherry tree. Cherries were getting ripe.

"Where are you going?" asked the General. "I don't know, sir." "What regiment do you belong to?" "I don't know, sir." "What do you know?" "I know that General Jackson said that we must not know anything till after the fight was over." "Is that all you know?" "I know I want to go to that cherry tree." "Well, go on." The next day, he came along and one of our men said to him: "General, where are you going?" He turned around and looked at him a few minutes and said: "Are you a good hand at keeping a secret?" "Yes, sir." "Well, so am I," and he rode on.

J. J. Stovall of Oglesby had a friend who ran and one who thought he was shot:

The battle of Jenkins' Ferry[19] was a hard-fought battle, and for a while we were in a very close place, so close that one of our men ran; and after the battle our Captain said; "Mike, what made you run?" He said: "Captain, because I could not fly." During this battle five of my company were shot down by my side—three on one side and two on the other side—and I tell you I felt as big as a bale of cotton. At this battle W. D. Jackson of Waco, Tex., was hit on the hollow of the thigh, and he hollered: "Stovall, I am killed. I am killed. Take my pocketbook and give it to my wife and tell her how I died." I went to examine his thigh and said; "No, you are not hurt, get up and come on." He said, "Yes, I am, I am bleeding to death." I assured him he was not bleeding; not even the skin was grazed.

William W. Stokey of Dallas was at Chickamauga[20] when camp was awakened by a stampeding Confederate artillery unit which they mistook for a Federal attack:

---

19 Jenkin's Ferry, Arkansas, April 30, 1864.

20 Chickamauga, Georgia, September 20, 1863.

From my vantage point, being the far side of an old stake and rider fence, to which I ran with an unseemly speed at the first outbreak of the inferno, I could see the other boys less fortunate and only half awake in their frantic efforts to get out of the way of what we all at first thought was a Yankee artillery or cavalry charge. I laugh till this day whenever I think of some of the ludicrous things I saw that night. I saw some of the boys climb impossible trees with agility, accuracy and speed of squirrels, while others struggled ten deep for the protection of a slender sapling trunk, while one poor fellow ran his cheek into one of the sharp projecting rails of the old stake and rider fence and with extraordinary good fortune missed inflicting upon himself serious injury. Another amusing little incident was a conversation which I over-heard between two of my comrades several feet away from me, behind a small tree trunk. One of them, my cousin D. W. Street, it appeared from the argument which carried to me above the turmoil, had been the first to reach the tree afore said, and the other fellow, whose name I have forgotten, had the incomparable gall to make a successful tackle and sepa-rate my cousin from first place at the sapling. It was then that I heard my cousin tell the other fellow, in no uncertain words, to "fade" (or words to that effect); that this was his tree, and immediately thereafter I saw the unknown hurled aside as my cousin resumed his position in a loving, embracing attitude next to the tree. At the same time I saw Lieut. Sandy Brown of Company E tear through a puddle of muddy water waist deep, he thinking that the water was white sand—there being several patches of this close about—and climb a tree with the agility of a monkey.

T. H. Stewart of McGregor reports on an officer who had his priorities straight:

At the battle of Cold Harbor[21] my First Lieutenant had just received a nice new hat from home. During the fight a ball struck the side of his head and cut quite a hole in his hat, besides giving him a severe flesh wound. At first we thought he was killed, but he soon began to rally, and looked up saying: "They ruined my hat, didn't they?" He bled so profusely that we had to take him to the rear. I saw him later in the afternoon and helped dress his head, which was still very bloody. I asked him how his hat was, and he said; "You fool, it is my head, and not my hat, that I am interested in."

Stewart also tells of another comrade at the Wilderness[22] who had an odd nickname:

At the battle of the Wilderness we had a man in our company named Taylor, whom we called "Puny," because of his immense size. He was about the biggest man in our regiment. On one occasion Puny kept dodging the bullets which were whizzing around his head, when Gen. Wolford said: "Puny, you ought not to do that. Just stand up and be a man." Just then a cannon ball cut some limbs from a tree just over the General's head and he fell flat off his horse. Puny said: "General, don't do that. Sit straight and be a man." The General replied: "Puny, you may dodge the big bullets, but let the little ones go."

J. G. Clark of Hico told of a comrade who had an interesting experience while on parole:

Comrade Albert Crawson was captured at Vicksburg[23] and paroled and went home. While at home he decided that he would go squirrel hunting, and taking up his old shot gun

---

21   Cold Harbor, Virginia. Battles were fought here on June 27, 1862, and June 1-3, 1864.

22   Battle of the Wilderness, Virginia, May 5-7, 1864.

23   Vicksburg, Mississippi, second campaign, April 1-July 4, 1863.

he proceeded into the woods and very unexpectedly to both himself and a Federal scout, they met, but Albert had the drop on the Federal, and threw his gun down on him. After looking each other in the eye for a moment, the Federal remarked; "Suppose you claim me as your prisoner." "No," said Crawson, "I wish it was so I could, but as I am a prisoner of war on parole, I can not take prisoners." Then said the scout "For God's sake take down that old gun I am tired of looking at the muzzle of it." Crawson laughingly complied with the request and after a few moments of conversation, the scout took Crawson's advice and headed back to his command.

Confusion was part of the war, and knowing when you were on the right side could even be a problem, as recorded by **Johnson Busbee Harris of Karnes City** at the battle of Holly Springs:[24]

There were three specially brave men who came under my observation in this fight. The one who held my horse, the one I found on picket, and a Federal, thinking he was with his own men, and realizing that the Yankees were routed, called to our men, "Fall in boys and we will whip the darn Rebels yet." When he realized where he was, he said: "By Gee, I'm in the wrong pew."

---

24 Holly Springs, Mississippi. Raid on December 20, 1862.

Over These Prison Walls
I Would Fly

There were two places a Confederate soldier did not want to go: the hospital and a prison camp. They figured their chances of survival were better on the field of battle than either one of those places. From the very beginning, a program of prisoner exchange was worked out. Neither side had the resources or the men to spare to maintain a proper prisoner of war facility, and death could come quickly in camp from stepping over the "dead line" or it could be a very slow process of disease and malnutrition. So escape was always on the Rebel mind, and probably the best of all these was **Private H. G. Damon of Corsicana** who served in Company D, Second Florida Infantry, Garland's Brigade, Longstreet's Corps, Army of Northern Virginia:

My prison experience began at Rock Island,[1] Ill. On the 19th day of September, just a little after dark, I escaped from the place through a cat hole under the fence, which I had enlarged with a case knife. Of the 15,000 or more prisoners confined at different times in Rock Island prison, I have the honor of being the only one who ever escaped this way. I waded from the island across the Mississippi to the Illinois shore, and walked up the railroad toward Chicago, laid in the woods next day, and on the next night boarded a train for

---

1   Rock Island Prison was located in the Mississippi River between the cities of Rock Island, Illinois, and Davenport, Iowa. About three miles long and a half-mile wide, it was very swampy and had poor drainage.

Chicago, riding part of the way between the cars, reaching Chicago next morning.

It may seen strange that Damon headed for Chicago instead of south, but he had a contact in Chicago, a Mrs. Judge Morris, who was hiding some Confederate soldiers who had come north to recruit for the Rebel army. But alas, along with the Rebel infiltrators, he was captured again and was sent to Camp Morton:[2]

The prison was rectangular in shape, and enclosed by a fence about twelve feet high. There was a walk on the outside of the fence, about three feet below the top, where the sentinels walked. These sentinels were about 100 feet apart. On the prison side of the fence were lamps with reflectors that threw such a bright light that you could see the smallest object 100 yards off. About ten feet from the fence was a ditch which was called the "dead line." The guards had orders to shoot any prisoner who attempted to cross that dead line. I had not been in Camp Morton long before I began to look for a chance to escape. The next day a Tennessee boy, named Dave Young, and I made the attempt, but were caught and came near being shot.

Damon and Young had their hands tied behind them and were tied to a post and ordered to mark time. Once when they came near stopping from exhaustion, the guard called, "Boys, I do not want to shoot you, but my orders are strict; you must keep on marking time." And so they did, for fifteen hours. But it did not deter his determination. The next escape plan was a little more elaborate:

We planned to charge the guards and escape over the wall. The success of this plan involved; first getting forty or

---

2   The 1860 Indiana State Fairgrounds at Indianapolis.

*fifty men who had the nerve to try it; second getting a suffi-
cient number of ladders to scale the 12-foot fence; third,
crossing a ditch six feet deep and several feet wide before getting to the wall; fourth, charging without weapons a guard
post on a high fence who would be sure to pour a volley of
shot into them, with the chance that several would be killed.
After due deliberation, we concluded to get up the crowd and
make that charge or die in the attempt.*

Damon's reminiscences seem to be a little confused about
whether or not the plan was his, for he later states that he
was sitting on his bunk getting ready to go to bed when someone reported the mob was making a charge on the fence.
Damon jumped up and ran to join the escape, but Dave
Young, still recalling the fifteen hours of marking time,
stayed in his bunk:

*When I got to No. 4 I saw our men behind the barracks
out of range of the guns of the guards. Some were in front
with ladders calling out rather feebly; "Come on, boys," while
those behind were saying with tremendous emphasis, "Go
ahead, boys." I said all they want is for some one to take the
lead, and I will do it. The memory of the fiendish and
un-merited cruelty that had been inflicted on me nerved me
and I rejoiced in an opportunity to lead a forlorn hope. In a
second I had made up my mind to lead that crowd, but I did
not get the chance. When I got within ten feet of the front the
foremost men made a dash and the whole crowd followed.*

The guards fired until their guns were empty and then tried
to keep the men off the fence with bayonets, but the mob was
frightening and the guards made a retreat themselves.
Wearing a citizen's suit, Damon walked through the little
town near the prison and soon made his way back south.

Private James F. Byrd of Robert Lee, who was captured when he disobeyed orders and dined with some young ladies, was sent to New Orleans and then to Ship Island, where he used a most unusual method to escape:

We were guarded by negroes and they made us carry wood for two or three miles on our shoulders. Finally the day came for the Fort Pillow[3] prisoners to be exchanged. They were marched out to within a short distance of where I was and halted. I watched the guard and when he was turned I stepped over among the officers who were to be exchanged. I told one of the officers that I was going to try to get away with them, and he told me that there was no chance as they had to go to headquarters and sign their paroles and that they would catch me and have me killed. I told him I was going to risk it any way. All was ready and we were marched to headquarters. I fell in right by the side of the officer with whom I had been in conversation. The officers were about through signing when the Colonel rode up and said that he wanted fourteen men to volunteer to carry rations aboard the boat. I was one of the first to volunteer, and shouldered a box of crackers and pulled for the boat. I found a staircase leading to the top of the boat, and up these steps I went. When at the top I took my seat among other soldiers who looked to be Confederates, and they proved to be part of the Fort Gaines[4] prisoners who had been left at New Orleans sick. The prisoners that I came down with started back to headquarters. I saw them halted, and I was afraid they had missed me. I was told afterwards that the Colonel said that he asked for fourteen men and that there was only thirteen.

---

3   Battle of Fort Pillow, Tennessee, took place on April 12, 1864.

4   Fort Morgan, Alabama, located on Mobile Point at the entrance to Mobile Bay. Battle fought August 5-23, 1864.

Some of the prisoners said this is all that came down and the guard seemed to be excited and said only thirteen came down. In the meantime, I had gone down into the hull of the boat and it was not very long until she pulled out for Mobile. It was only a short time until the officer with whom I had talked came down, and he started to say something of my escape (of which he was very proud) and I told him to be careful not to be seen talking to me that I might be discovered.

Richard Johnson Barbour of Normangee expressed the displeasure of most of the Southerners who were guarded by negro troops:

I lost my right arm at Hatcher's Run[5] on Weldon Road. Was taken prisoner after losing my arm and sent to Fortress Monroe,[6] where I was guarded and cursed by negro soldiers and suffered all manner of indignities.

Capt. A. B. Barnes of Greenville was another of those daring Rebels who chanced life itself in order to escape the rigors of prison life. The prison he was placed in had a smallpox epidemic with from six to ten prisoners dying each day, which was brought on by poor sanitation and overcrowding:

I was captured Jan. 6, 1862, and was in prison in Alton, Ill.,[7] fifty-six days and escaped March 6, 1862, in the following way: An old dutchman was employed to haul water from the Mississippi River to the prison, and it was the duty of the prisoners to unload the water from the large barge to the

---

5   Battle of Hatcher's Run, Virginia, on Febuary 5 through 7, 1865. Also known as Armstrong's Mill, Boydton Plank Road, Dabney's, Illinois, and Vaughan Road.

6   Fort Monroe, Virginia.

7   Former Illinois abandoned state penitentiary, was reopened as a prison camp in 1862.

smaller ones. On this occasion I was left to finish the unloading and when the last was out and the sentinel was just returning on his beat I jumped into the barrel and was carried off towards the river. When well down to the river I jumped out and, disguised by a heavy citizen's overcoat and with a half smoked cigar in my mouth, no one supposed I was an escaped prisoner. I made my way to the depot, and with fifty cents, my last change, I bought a ticket to St. Louis, Mo., and was soon amongst friends. I don't know what went with the Dutchman.

J. V. Carter of Voca, like so many others, came out of prison with his life changed forever:

.... was under Gen. A. Hill[8] until the battle of Gettysburg,[9] where we were captured and sent to Fort Delaware[10] on July 1, 1863. We were put in line and marched thirty miles a day. At 10 o'clock Gen. Hill fainted and fell on the road, which delayed the column fifteen minutes. When night came on we were put in a corral and guarded and the next day reached Baltimore and were put in what seemed to be a stock yard. We were kept there until the morning of the 5th of July, when we were put on a canal boat and run down to Delaware Bay and put on Delaware Island. We got there in July and they said that our crew made 13,000 on the island at the time. A few days later they shipped a great many to Lookout Point,[11] but left enough on the island to average thirty deaths a day for more than a year. At first they were buried without any clothes on at all, but the last six months they were buried

---

8   Ambrose Powell Hill.

9   Gettysburg, Pennsylvania, July 1-3, 1863.

10   Pea Patch Island in the Delaware River.

11   The largest prison in the North, established August 1, 1863 at Point Lookout, Maryland.

with underwear on. They kept thirty men on detail to dig graves. We had one blanket to each two men and two hardtacks and one cup of soup twice a day. I could not have lived on such rations. I made rings and kept up until I took sick. I lay eighteen weeks in the hospital on Delaware Island. I had to take the oath of "allegiance" before they would let me come home. I had bone scurvy and could only walk with crutches.

Lewis Cash of Forney spent twenty-one months in prison at Fort Delaware:

. . . . . . had two hardtacks at a meal. The weather was cold and I suffered all the time I was there, as we had only one blanket to the man.

Archibald Gray Adams of Marshall, captured at Fort Donelson,[12] found things a lot better at Johnson's Island prison:

On Johnson's Island[13] the prisoners were well treated and given plenty to eat. Each comrade took his turn at cooking, but not always with great success. Many of the boys amused themselves by making various articles of jewelry inlaid with gutta-percha,[14] which articles were highly treasured by these same boys.

Adams was moved by a dream he had while in prison that seemed to foretell the battle of Shiloh,[15] although he had the wrong river:

While in prison I dreamed one night that there was a battle on the Mississippi River, and the Confederates beat the

---

12 Fort Donelson, Tennessee, February 13-16, 1862.

13 Johnson's Island Prison, Ohio, in Sandusky Bay on Lake Erie.

14 Substance obtained from the sap of trees.

15 Shiloh (Pittsburg Landing), Tennessee, April 6-7, 1862.

Yanks and drove them into the river under the gunboats. I got up the next morning and was telling my dream when my comrades announced "that was too good to be true, come and take your beating." So they laid me on the "cooling board" and gave me a dressing. Short time after, received news of Shiloh.

T. H. Adkisson of Dublin wanted nothing to do with prison and was willing to put his life on the line to avoid confinement in a Northern stockade:

Was wounded in the leg at Missionary Ridge.[16] Was wounded at Jonesboro[17] on Aug. 31, 1864 in the left arm. I was taken prisoner twice, but got away on the grounds that I did not want to go North, and took chances on running. The Yankees shot my hat off, but I got away just the same.

And **Joseph E. Bonner of Whitney** avoided prison by staying true to his pledge:

I made a pledge upon entering the army that I would never gamble, be taken to a hospital, sick or wounded; or surrender. I carried out my pledge. I was ordered to surrender twice, but thought of my pledge and took my chance of escape.

Irby Holt Boggess of Saint Joe was wounded only once but in strange places: prison and the buttocks:

I was wounded only once and a cowardly guard bayoneted me in the hip because I did not obey orders readily.

T. A. Foster of Canyon City was marched to Cumberland Gap where his officers surrendered the command to the Federals about the twenty-third of September, 1863:

---

16   Missionary Ridge, Tennessee, November 25, 1863.

17   Jonesborough, Georgia, August 31 and September 1, 1864.

Was taken to Camp Douglas where we remained for over twenty-one months. While in prison I made pocket knifes and trinkets of all kinds which furnished me some money to buy necessities. From there was taken to New Orleans where after about ten days, we were paroled at Natchez, Mississippi by a Colonel commanding a negro regiment. I returned home June 23, 1865. I was never in a hard battle during the war and escaped without a wound. As to my treatment while in prison I suppose I should not complain. I have worked thirty days for a hat and my rations consisted of a pint of "hog food." Our food was cooked in a ninety-five gallon kettle which was supposed to hold enough for a day's rations which was composed of beef, bread, and beans all stirred together and then each man was given a cupful. This was all we got and I have seen men shot down while trying to steal a bone from the slop barrel to gnaw on.

Colville Edmondson Young of Forreston, whose nickname was Tobe, just couldn't seem to stay out of trouble, even at home in Fayetteville, Tennessee, where there were about as many Yankees as there were Rebels:

For a private, I had a rollicking big time, always with something to eat and to spare; barefooted and ragged, never missed a march or a fight from Seven Pines[18] to Gettysburg, where they got me in the right "wing" and sent me to Delaware. Not liking my fare, I jumped my board bill, ate green apples eleven days; got back to my regiment; got a furlough home. Carried letters home for the boys and found that my mother and sisters had been badly treated, having been in prison. One sister and a neighbor woman still there. Got into a fight.

---

18   Seven Pines (Fair Oaks), May 31 through June 1, 1862.

On furlough, Tobe was captured and taken to Nance's Mill and then to the hospital at Pulaske and then to the stockade at Tullahoma, Tennessee:

I found my sister and Mrs. Burrow Malear prisoners because they would not ride with the Yankee officers as escorts, and though they were sent home, I was tried for murder, robbery, and for being a spy; and upon the testimony of Dan Cobb, a negro, and some deserters was convicted. They killed four of their own men and said that I did it. Was tried by a military commission and was condemned to be hanged. Mother got me a reprieve; was exchanged; and got home.

Scheduled to hang on Friday, his mother fought for his life. Then Governor Andrew Johnson arrived on Wednesday, having been out of the state:

My mother and her friends went to the capitol. At length Mrs. White went in to make her appeal. She recited the story, her own beauty no doubt adding to the effectiveness of her persuasion. When the document was handed to my mother, she went at once to the St. Cloud hotel and was admitted alone. Glancing at the paper, the official swore. My mother was then given a paper by Gov. Johnson and admonished to go at once to Washington and to give the papers to no one except the President. Much red tape had to be passed, but at last she stood in the presence of Mr. Lincoln. She was too weak and over strung, and all she could say was; "My son; my son!"

It took another visit to Lincoln's office before he was convinced Tobe was a regular soldier and not a bushwhacker, but finally he said:

Cheer up; cheer up. There is brightness in the world, and there may be a share for you.

By the president's pardon, Tobe became a prisoner of war and was exchanged, but the strain had been too much for his mother. Soon after her return from Washington, she passed away. Tobe was seventeen years old when he joined the Confederate army and nineteen when he was wounded at Gettysburg.

In his memoirs, Tobe elaborated on his escape from the prison on Pea Patch Island (Fort Delaware) in the Delaware River:

My escape from prison at Fort Delaware. We were good swimmers, and practiced till we thought we could float. We got a plank and tied our clothes to it. It was agreed that each was to take care of himself and was to make no appeal to the others, dying if must be, without a call for help. On the night of Aug. 12, 1863. We floated on for an hour or more and felt a sensation which encouraged us to carry out our plans. Soon the wind rose and the waves ran high, and the passing of a steamer brought us great danger. The names of this crew were Tom Stewart, John McKinney, James Casion, George Stonebreaker, John Moore and myself. John being weak, lost his hold on the board and was drifting away, but, true to his promise, uttered not a word. I saw his situation and asked him if he could regain his hold on the board, and he said, "No, I'm gone;" but I got the others to help me and we got him back. After a stay of about six hours in the water we reached Newcastle. We pulled our frail bark ashore and on untying our clothes I found that mine were missing. John, realizing what he owed me, offered me his, but the offer was declined, as I thought I would present fully as good an appearance with the limited wardrobe as he. We went four miles before we found anyone from whom we could risk asking assistance, but found a man who clothed us and gave us breakfast,

*dinner and supper and passed us over the Newcastle River
and gave us his blessing. Without unusual incident we
reached the Susquehanna River, where we appropriated a
yawl; but there were no oars and the crossing was with much
difficulty. John, being weak could not have held on but for
my help. We crossed, however, and then the next river was
the Potomac, and then there was something to eat. Then
came Culpepper C. H., Orange C. H., and then the regiment.
We were nothing but skeletons, but our patriotism was just
the same.*

Solomon Thomas Blessing of Fort Worth was able to give
up an old habit while in prison:

*Prison cured me of the tobacco habit, because there was
none to chew.*

But he was not happy with the water supply or the bill of fare:

*The rations issued the prisoners was sufficient in quan-
tity, but two or three times a week we had salt fish and water
was very scarce. The twelve wells inside the dead line yielded
only about a quart each twenty-four hours to the man, and
salt cod was freely offered in exchange for water.*

E. K. Hillyer of Ennis had nothing good to say about prison
provisions:

*When Grant opposed the exchange of prisoners he said
that it was cheaper to feed them than to fight them. He meant
that it was cheaper to starve them than to fight them. There
was no excuse for the starving of our prisoners as they were
starved. It has been said that the petty officers sold the provisions which the government furnished for us. Perhaps so, we
never got them.*

William Hugh Graham of Athens gives a little insight into
what prison life was like. He was captured in Arkansas when

the Yankees came up the river and surprised them in winter quarters:

The enemy came up the Arkansas River in gunboats and transports above and below us and began to shell and close upon us from all sides, as they had about fifteen or twenty to our one. We held our ground for two days. After our surrender our troubles began. We were crowded on transports like cattle and sent up the Mississippi River in as cold weather as I ever saw, with but little clothing, fire or blankets, to Camp Douglas, Ill. We were placed in barracks about 16x35, containing about 125 men. Here we were kept about three months with one blanket and thirteen pounds of hay for bedding, with almost nothing to eat, and great numbers died from exposure; but they died heroes, and were just as good men as those who lived through the war or fell on the field of battle. Sometime in May we were started to Richmond, Va., to be exchanged. It was then that we could sing "Dixie" and "Home Sweet Home" with the spirit and understanding, for we would rather bare our breast on the field of battle than to live in a Federal prison.

B. M. Thompson of Glen Rose confirms the report on the conditions at Camp Douglas:

At Arkansas Post[19] after a hard struggle we were overpowered by Grant's army, taken prisoner and sent to Camp Douglas, Chicago, Ill., where some of our men froze to death the first night.

Curtis Green of Leon Junction, caught with a Yankee overcoat on, faced death by firing squad as a spy and thus risked his life to escape:

---

19 Arkansas Post, Arkansas, January 10-11, 1863.

On the 23d of September I was captured in a blue uniform and taken to Rome, Ga. and placed in a log calaboose and the next morning handcuffed. The third day I was carried before about six Yankee officers. There witnesses appeared against me. One was a deserter from our company, then belonging to the First (Yankee) Alabama Calvary, commanded by Col. Spencer. The others were two women whose husbands had deserted from our army. They stated that I was Curtis Green, and belonged to the Sixteenth Georgia Calvary, and was known to be a secret scout.

Green does not admit to being a spy or explain why he was dressed in Union blue, but he soon learned that his sentence was death:

On the fifth day I received a note from a young lady by the name of Reynolds, through her brother, who was in prison with me at the time, telling me to get out or die in the attempt, as I was condemned as a spy and my doom was death. I then went to cutting on the double floor to make a hole through which I might escape. I had been allowed an old spade to build a fire on, by which to smoke the mosquitoes out, and I turned the fire over and burned the floor and burned my cuttings, so that it was disguised. The next morning the spade was taken from me. It was Sunday, Oct. 3. The guard was changed every two hours, and the watch in the door gave me notice of the guard relief, when I would spread my blanket over the hole and lie down on it. The sergeant of the guard would count us fourteen Confederate boys, put his guard, and retire. I would then uncover and begin whittling again and continue for the next two hours till I had notice of the relief guard. I continued this way all day, and about ten minutes before 8 o'clock that night I had my hole completed. I waited till the new relief was put on so that I might have two

hours to get out of town. When the relief was put on I told the
Yankee sentinel I wanted to sing to him a song. He told me to
get up and sit in the door and sing. I did so, and it was as
follows:

> O dreadful, dark and rainy night
> How have my joys passed away?
> The sun's gone down, and this day is past,
> And now I am going home at last.
>
> O Lord, what will become of me?
> I am condemned to die (as all can see).
> To heaven or hell my soul shall fly
> All in a moment when I die.
>
> Judge Daniel has my sentence passed;
> These prison walls I leave at last.
> No one to cheer my dropped head
> Until I am numbered with the dead.

You have to wonder if Curtis had a hard time keeping a
straight face as he sang to the guards, knowing that in a few
moments he would be gone:

When I had sung my song to the sentinels they were
dumbfounded and did not speak a word for two minutes, but
gave me eulogy for singing the song, as they said I was condemned to die. I laid down on my pallet and kicked the boys,
and they got up making a fuss looking for water, as it was
understood they should do while I was making a fuss going
through the floor. I was then in a garden which guarded the
calaboose. I ran to the back side of the garden and jerked off
two palings, went through and ran around nearly in front of
the calaboose, some fifty or sixty yard away, got a plank
1x12x8 foot long, went down the sewer into the Osstanaula
River about the old Horter bridge place and swam down the
river to Etowah River, then down the Coosa River and
landed on the Widow Billup's farm. I have always said that I

swam two and one-half miles, but have believed it was further; but I did not want to exaggerate. I had a piece of soap and soaped my hands, which were much drawn up from being in the water, pulled off the handcuffs, then pulled off my clothes and wrung them out. I was in my sock feet, having left my boots in the calaboose. I then started for home.

Another escape, reported by **John P. Hale of Farmersville,** was from Rock Island and surprised one negro guard:

Some of the boys decided they would get out, so they began tunneling the prison, next to the fence, and finally got outside. The negro man who was on guard, said, "Praise the Lawd; jes look at de men comin' out o' de groun." They were fired into and one was wounded, two captured and four got away.

J. F. Hardy of Marlin was captured at the battle of Nashville[20] on December 15, 1864:

The Yanks were very cruel to us, also. Our sleeping apartments were (in a long barrack) on bunks, three in a row, one above the other, and only one blanket to the man. When the lights were put out, we were not even permitted to speak to our bunk-mate, and if the Yanks caught a fellow talking after dark, he was taken out and placed on Morgan's mule, regardless of the weather. Morgan's mule was a 2x4 scantling put up on legs about ten feet high. So you see, a fellow would get very cold while he was taking his ride. I had to ride the wooden horse one day myself. There were about fifteen thousand prisoners there, and we were very thick, and the Yankees would beat some of the boys with a big walking stick like they were dogs. We were not treated as soldiers, fighting for a just cause.

---

20 Nashville, Tennessee, December 15-16, 1864.

F. M. Martin of Oglesby gives a count on the number of deaths that seems high until you consider the fact that about 26,500 Confederate soldiers died in prison camps:

I was captured and sent to Camp Douglas, where I was almost starved. Out of 12,000 Confederates in that prison, only 7,000 were turned out alive. I ate my rations at one meal, and went till next day before I got any more. All kinds of punishments were inflicted upon prisoners.

Johnson Busbee Harris of Karnes City never went to prison because he was able to dupe a Federal soldier into believing a boy from Mississippi was afraid of a mule:

The Federals came up unexpectedly and took me captive. It was only for a short one for me, though. My captor, with his pistol in hand, made me lead the way to the barn. In the stable was a fine mule. He ordered me to go in the stable and catch the mule. I refused. Told him I was afraid of a mule. At last exasperated, he rushed in and grabbed the mule. It was only for a moment, but it sufficed for me to escape.

But even when captured and on their way to prison, the Rebel spirit was hard to quench, as **T. H. Holloway of Odell** told in his memoirs:

At Murfreesboro[21] I was given a detail to take a captured battery of six guns out to our lines, but owing to the dense smoke we were surrounded and captured. On our way to prison many of the prisoners had their feet and hands frostbitten. Two escaped before getting to Chicago and two (Apperson and Hendricks) died in prison. On the boat taking us to prison were 800 prisoners. We stopped in St. Louis, and we were marched up to the city and formed in two lines

---

21 Murfreesboro (Stone's River), Tennessee, December 31 through January 2, 1863.

facing a two-story hotel where the officer in charge made us a speech, promising us liberty, anywhere inside the lines, if we would take the "Oath of Allegiance." When he was through he ordered all who would take advantage of the offer to step two paces to the front. The proudest moment of my war experience was when only two of the 800 ragged, starved and frozen bunch stepped to the front. The several ladies, who were on the upstairs porch, waved their handkerchiefs and cried out "Stand to your colors, God bless you, we love to see you do it!" Then came up out of that two feet of snow the "Rebel Yell" from those 800 throats, and a loud huzza for "Jeff Davis and the Southern Confederacy." Our answer to the Yankees was that we would rot and starve before we would take the oath, and many did.

William Gentry of Anson accidently walked into a Yankee picket line and, since he was wearing a blue coat, was fortunate not to be shot as a spy. At Douglas prison he reported:

Here I was robbed of all I had except a change of clothing and one light blanket. Two of us would occupy one bunk with one blanket to cover with and one for a bed, with no fire at night. In this cold state our rations were one-fourth pound of poor beef and one tablespoonful of navy beans and a third of a loaf of bread per day. After I had been here awhile some friend of mine got me a position as cook. This was like being elected the Governor of Texas.

James E. Lodsdon of Gainesville, as was the case with most of the Southern boys, did not like being under the command of negroes:

They furnished our rations ready cooked, which consisted of one pint of bacon soup, four ounces of pickled beef and four crackers for one day. The next day would be one pint of mush, four ounces of pickled pork and four crackers, alternation that way the whole time we were there. The prisoners had to keep the cook houses supplied with wood, which had to be carried seven miles. A detail of prisoners was sent out every morning with a string of "nigger" soldiers on each side, and each prisoner had to bring back two sticks of cord wood.

In prison, keeping warm and well was important, but according to **W. L. McCandless of Farmersville,** food was still the greatest need:

Was taken prisoner in December, 1862, and sent to Rock Island, Ill., where I stayed eighteen months and ate dog.

And according to **Andrew Jackson Meers of Austin,** who was imprisoned on Johnson Island, eating dog was just the beginning:

Men of high rank ate house cats and rats and other stuff too revolting to mention and men visited the swill barrel in search of something to eat.

J. H. Parish of Wolfe City expressed it best for all those who were confined in prison:

After my capture was sent to Ft. Delaware, where I remained for twenty-two months. The suffering in this prison was great. Was captured July 3rd, 1863, and was released May 31, 1865. I would prefer two years in the front ranks to spending the same length of time in prison. We prisoners had the opportunity of taking the oath of allegiance and as we refused, our clothing and rations were taken away from us.

Captured at Gettysburg, **Wm. Henry Mathews of Livingston** reported on prison cruelty:

At the battle of Gettysburg on July 3, 1863, our Texas Brigade charged the heights of Little Round Top and as we were advancing up the side of the mountain, it was very steep and rocky from our starting point, and the distance so great and the heat so excessive, that when we reached the enemy's line we were all exhausted, and could go no further. We advanced to within fifty yards of their line and fell behind large rocks. I fell behind a rock about eighteen inches high and fired one shot and began to reload lying down, and while holding up my gun for the powder to fall to the bottom was shot in the arm, but I am thankful to say, that it was not broken. Our Captain, R. W. Hubert, with seventeen others, was made prisoners at this place......After being captured, I with a large number of others, was sent to Ft. Delaware where my brother was killed and where we remained for twenty-three months. The guard that killed my brother at Fort Delaware prison was what we called galvanized Yanks. He first enlisted in our army and later joined the Federals. This man's name was Smith, from Flint Hill, Mo. I feel that I can never forgive him. As to our treatment in prison they gave us only three ordinary crackers per day, with a small piece of beef or bacon about the size of an egg.

J. H. McDonald of Commerce was also captured at Gettysburg and sent to Fort Delaware and reported on the most common cause of death in camp:

Was taken prisoner the 1st day of July, 1863, at Gettysburg and carried to Fort Delaware. I stayed there twenty-three months and eleven days. Twenty-two of our company were carried there and four died. We did not get half rations and only one blanket to the man. I came near freezing but I kept well with the exception of smallpox. There were about a thousand cases of smallpox there at one time......I would have preferred to have been with the company, but you see they preferred to half feed us rather than to fight us.

An idea of what prison fare was like can be seen in the testimony of **Homer V. McMickle of Lufkin**:

When I was captured I weighed 158 pounds, and when I was released I weighed 85 pounds. I came near to starving and would have done so but for the help of others whose people at home sent them money. Several did die of starvation. The day of Lincoln's death we were not allowed to speak to each other nor for thirty days afterwards. It is useless to say we did not steal something to eat when we had the chance, and when caught we were punished by being hung up by the thumbs till we fainted, or death would end our sufferings.

Edward C. Perry of Wills Point, like all the others, described the hardness of prison:

At Arkansas Post, after two days' hard fighting they took us in and put us on three transports and sent us up to Camp Chase,[22] Columbus, Ohio, where we stayed four months. We arrived there in the night and marched four miles out to the prison. The snow was ten inches deep, and they took us two at a time and searched us, taking everything we had, clothes, money, pocket knives, and pictures, and when the last ones got in next morning they were nearly frozen. We went there in cattle cars. We were transferred from there to Fort Delaware, where we stayed three weeks, and were then sent to City Point, Va., and exchanged at Petersburg.

Perry spent a little time at Richmond before he returned to the service at Chattanooga and fought with Gen. Bragg, Gen. Joseph E. Johnston, and Gen. Hood, when he was captured again at the battle of Franklin:

---

22 Camp Chase, Ohio, on the outskirts of Columbus.

I was captured and sent to Johnson's Island, Lake Erie, where I stayed with 3000 other Confederate officers for eight months. Was paroled in June, 1865, and came back to my home in Harrison County Texas, after four years and two months of war and bloodshed. Was in the hospital only four days in the whole four years. At Johnson's Island our rations were a loaf of bread and a piece of pickled pork about an inch square, which was devoured as soon as divided at the mess hall, and most of the boys ate it at one meal and went hungry till the next day. Sunday's rations were issued Saturday, and most of the boys ate what they got and went over till Monday for the next meal. There were sixty-five men to one room with one very small stove with about half enough wood, and it was the coldest winter I ever saw. A barrel of water was brought in every morning, but the lake froze over to Sandusky, three miles, and everything was brought over on the ice.

Wesley McDonald of Atlanta told of the deprivations during the trip to prison:

After recovering from my wound so I could walk a little and being in the hands of the enemy, I was sent with a good many other prisoners from Iuka, Miss., to Columbus, Ky., where we were placed on a steamboat. These boats were taken up the river to Cairo, Ill., where they were repaired and then started to Vicksburg to exchange us. When we got to Vicksburg or within a few miles of it, the authorities would not permit the flag of truce to enter, so they carried us back to Alton, Ill., and put us in the old penitentiary where I remained for three months in the dead of winter. No use to tell how much I suffered there. I will return to the boat. There was I suppose, about one thousand prisoners on board, and we lay on the large piles of coal on deck or anywhere we could crouch down trying to keep from freezing. One young man, a messmate of mine about twenty years old, by the name of William Barlow, while we were anchored near Vicksburg, gave a cough and fell dead right by my side. On the way up the river I saw several prisoners jump off the boat to swim ashore. I saw one crawl up the bank after a dozen shots had been fired at him by the guards. Another succeeded in reaching the shore but as we passed on, we saw that he was on an island. This was in November and the weather very cold. I was kept in this prison for three months to a day and then exchanged at City Point, VA. I had several bad spells of sickness during the war, and am very thankful that the Lord has spared my life to write this little sketch.

J. F. Smith of Morgan had nothing good to say about prison or the Yankees, but he found a way to make an honest dollar, even in prison:

I was taken prisoner at Fort Gibson[23] and carried to Alton, Ill., where many a poor fellow went out a corpse. This hideous prison had been condemned as unfit for their own prisoners but was good enough for us. Over a thousand prisoners were confined in this horrible place, which swarmed with vermin of every description, and as hard as the Yankees were to contend with, these were the worst. There was no chance to whip them nor to retreat. As bad as was our fare, we told the Yankees we would rot before we would take the oath. I made jewelry in the way of breast pins and rings, of Gutta-Percha, and inlaid them with gold and sold them through the guards to the people in town, who were anxious to have anything made by a rebel prisoner.

---

23 Fort Gibson, Indian Territory. Under siege in September of 1864.

But **A. J. Smith of Temple** found a way out, even with a horrible handicap:

Was taken prisoner four times, making my escape each time. The longest that they kept me was eight days, and that was after I had lost my leg. I made my escape that time by the assistance of Miss Jinnie Bell and Miss Ludie Brothers. They brought me a cannon ball to knock the guard down with. He was a negro, and I hit him hard enough to have killed him, and made my way to the river. When safe I felt like I was promoted to the highest rank by a couple of young ladies. I would like for the world to know what risk they took of losing their lives in giving me liberty. Miss Bell married Jim Neal of Lebanon, Tenn., and Miss Brothers married Jim Kirk of near the same place. I hope that their children will know how brave and noble their mothers were.

James H. Polk of Fort Worth tells of how the Confederate prisoners were put under fire by the Yankees:

I was one of the immortal 600 officers sent to Morris' Island and as a matter of retaliation were put under fire of Confederate Batteries, where for forty-two days we remained under fire of our own guns. We were transported on a filthy cattle ship, and four men were allowed the space 4x6 feet. We were nineteen days on this floating purgatory before landing on Morris' Island. Our rations on Morris' Island was ten ounces of rotten corn meal and one pint of salt pickle per day. We were accorded the most brutal treatment ever received by prisoners of war and the death rate was very heavy till January 1865.

J. B. Sutton of McGregor tells a little of the inhumanity of prison guards, too numerous to mention, but gives the Yankee officers the benefit of the doubt:

I was taken prisoner the last time at Charleston,[24] *Tenn., under the gallant Joe Wheeler, as brave and honorable a General as the sun ever shone upon. I was sent to Rock Island, Ill., where I was held fourteen months, and it would be horrible to try to relate all the abuses which were heaped on us by the brutal guards. The higher officers may not have known all this, and it would have been suicidal for us to have reported our treatment.*

Alexander Walker of Hico goes into a little more detail of the treatment of prisoners at Rock Island:

Rock Island was a nice prison at first, and we were given plenty to eat for the first eight or ten months. There were ten thousand prisoners there at one time, and we were guarded by old soldiers, and they treated us well; but the remainder of the seventeen months we were there grub was very scarce, and we were guarded by negroes and the sixty-day troops and we were badly treated. I was told that there were about 2,100 Confederates prisoners buried there. I was released about the 25th of June, and was sent home via St. Louis and Memphis, Tenn. When we got a paper which was called "The Copperhead" they would stop the rations till the paper was produced. Their mode of punishing Confederates was to tie them up by the thumbs. They quit that and made them "ride Morgan's mare," which was a 2x4 scantling with the edges beveled.

At least one Confederate, **W. M. T. Thompson of Austin**, found a constructive way to do his time in prison:

The inmates of the prison, finding out that I was an old teacher, insisted that I teach them. They were all young men

---

24 Skirmishes took place here in November and December of 1863 and
    August 18, 1864.

from 16 to 22 years old, and some had never been to school. I promised that I would if we could get some books. The third day some ladies from Baltimore visited us and promised the books. Those noble ladies fulfilled their promise and those young prisoners began to learn how to spell, read, write, and cipher under their fellow prisoner.

Robert Agustus Brantley of Summerville refused to take the "oath" and remained in prison until the end of the war:

I was taken prisoner at Gettysburg on the second day, and was taken to Fort Delaware, where I remained twenty-three months. There were great cards placed on the wall offering $1,000 to any one who would take the oath and join the Union Army. Two regiments of deserters were made up there. We were told that they afterwards deserted and the place cards were torn down. All the Confederates who took this oath were afterwards taken to separate barracks and given three meals per day as their reward.

A. B. Foster of Comanche also refused to take the oath, and he tells of the suffering of those who preferred prison to compromise:

I was taken to Chattanooga and put in an old jail with a fence around it and held for several days, offering us our freedom if we would take the "Oath of Allegiance to the United States." Those who took the oath were taken across the Ohio River, but the most of us refused it and went to prison at Camp Chase. I was put in the barracks sometime in September, 1864, and we were retaliated on the condition of the Andersonville Prison in Georgia, and from that time on till the 14th of March, I was hungry all the time. We talked all day about something to eat and dreamed about it at night. I see from the Confederate Veteran that we lost 2,260 Confederate prisoners at Camp Chase and how it was that all did not die I can not see. Often men would die on their bunks at night and their bedfellow would know nothing of it till morning. I have often thought that if it were to do over again I would take the oath and get out, but I thought of the request of my dying brother. Disease of every kind, small pox, pneumonia, and erysipelas,[25] anything, kills men easily when they are already half starved.

Another who refused to take the oath was **Marcellu B. Fuqua of Sulphur Springs**:

Was captured Feb. 29, 1864, and taken to the old Capital Prison at Washington, D.C., remaining there until the 14th of June and transferred to Fort Delaware and was released on June 14, 1865. You will observe from the above dates that I was in prison about fifteen and a half months. This I consider the most patriotic service I rendered the Confederacy —to say nothing about the many engagements our company had with the enemy in 1863. I could have taken the oath any time after I was captured and been free, but I preferred to remain a prisoner with all the horrors of a Federal prison than to disgrace my cause and myself and did not take the oath until every vestige of the Confederacy had surrendered.

---

25 An acute infectious disease characterized by fever and chills and a rapidly spreading brilliant red inflammation of the skin caused by a streptococcus.

Bravado and Valor

What made men charge up a hill toward a stone wall bristling with enemy muskets and cannon? Why would a man with family waiting at home volunteer for a mission that meant certain death? Perhaps we will never understand the Rebel mind. The devotion to the Southland was only overshadowed by their love of their home state. True, not all were brave and daring, and many even ran at the first burst of battle. But the stories of Southern men who willingly gave their own lives for their country and their fellow soldiers is endless.

Mrs. Sue McLemore of Winnesboro reported for **W. H. Ashcroft of Sulphur Springs**, whose nickname was Mat:

Mat Ashcroft while in the trenches defending Atlanta,[1] made the offer of his life for his comrade, J. A. Weaver. The siege of Atlanta was long and hard; often the soldiers were half starved and poorly clad. The enemy's picket had been drawing nearer and nearer our soldiers and ammunition was running short. Unfortunately, the ordinance wagon was beyond a hill quite a distance from where that part of the army was stationed. Col. J.A. Weaver was in command of the brigade, as Col. W. D. Ector had been wounded. The General in command of the division sent an order to Col. Weaver to send a man for ammunition. He did, but the man never got there. He sent another, who shared the fate of the other sent out. Then the Division Commander ordered Col. Weaver again to send for ammunition. Col. Weaver replied that he

---

1   Atlanta, Georgia, July 22, 1864.

could not sacrifice his men, for it was instant death to go. Again the order came. Col. Weaver determined not to sacrifice his men but called for volunteers and stepped forward himself and made preparations to go on what he believed a death journey. Instantly there sprang from the rank, Mat Ashcroft, who said, "No, Col. Weaver, you are needed here, and your wife and children need you at home, I will go." At this time Bob Nelson came forward and was standing by the side of Mat, as much as to say he was going, too. Col. Weaver begged them not to go, but he (Nelson) said if Ashcroft went he would go, too; that at this critical hour their Colonel must not be sacrificed. Mat outlined his plan to the Colonel. Near the crest of the hill stood a tree. His plan was as they rose they would place their hats on the bayonets and draw the enemy's fire and rush over. They bade their comrades good-bye. Mat asked his Colonel if he never returned to take a message to his mother, and commended her to his care. It was with an aching heart their comrades saw them go, as they thought, to death, but the ruse succeeded. Their hats drew the enemy's fire and they rushed across. How anxiously did Col. Weaver and their comrades watch for their return. After a long wait they saw the hats slowly come across the crest of the hill. Was it possible they would fool the enemy again? As they neared the tree the enemy fired again, and from the jaws of death rushed the two boys loaded with ammunition, and the army was saved for the present. There was silence for a few moments when their comrades realized they were safe. Col. Weaver met them, but was too full for utterance. They had offered their lives for him. Suddenly a mighty roar as it swept down that vast army of soldiers, until the very heaven sent back the echo of those grateful hearts. It is said that when the enemy saw the bravery of those two boys that they cheered, too. When the U.C.V.[2] Camp was organized in Sulphur Springs it was named Mat Ashcroft.

Even at the highest level, the Confederate soldier, willing to give his own life, protected his leaders as **John Allison of Marquez** recalled at the battle of the Wilderness:[3]

We next met the enemy at the Wilderness. It was here that Gen. Lee rode up to our regiment and said, "What command is this?" When we told him it was Hood's Texas Brigade, he said, "I will go in the fight with the Texas Brigade." A man stepped out of ranks and told Lee to go to the rear, that he might be killed, and our country could not afford to lose him. He rode slowly back to the rear, and in a few moments the fight began.

John D. Keith of Santa Anna was the gunner on "Whistling Dick"[4] at Vicksburg and recalled an incident of bravery by a fellow Confederate:

In 1862, while fighting Farragut's[5] fleet, two of our men, while seriously wounded, begged piteously for water, and one of them said to Dave Dickson; "Won't you give me a drink?" To do this was to risk being killed, as the air was full of shot and shell. Dave said: "If I live long enough, I will." He took a canteen and deliberately walked seventy-five yards directly toward the enemy to an old cistern, drew the water and returned in the same deliberate way and gave his dying

---

2   United Confederate Veteran's Camp.

3   Battle of the Wilderness, Virginia, May 5 through 7, 1864.

4   "Whistling Dick" was an 18-pounder cannon used at Vicksburg by Confederates whose conical projectiles produced a distinctive whistling sound in flight. Keith reports that he held this position until "she was bursted."

5   David Glasgow Farragut, USN.

friend a drink. I have often thought that this was one of the most daring and heroic deeds and proof of devotion to a comrade that occurred during the war.

Most of the veterans who were at Fishing Creek[6] when General Zollicoffer[7] was killed make note of it in their memoirs, and **Will Ed. Kelly of Cedar Creek** was no exception, but he also remembered another officer who took an unusual way of threatening the Yankees:

One incident came under my observation at the battle of Chickamauga.[8] Our commanding officer, Major Coon, was riding up and down the line shouting to the Yankees at the top of his voice that if they shot him he would report them to Susie Coon.

Kelly did not reveal who Susie was, but obviously Major Coon assumed the Yankees did.

W. H. Hudson of Edna gives an account of an officer who refused to obey orders given by a unnamed general at Pleasant Hill[9] to charge an enemy battery, which was supported by three solid lines of infantry entrenched in ditches some thirty or forty yards apart:

Col. Buchel, an officer of acknowledged ability and bravery on the field of battle, knowing the foolishness of such a charge, refused to take his men into such a trap. The General referred to, ordered him for the second time, and accused him of cowardice. Colonel Buchel told him that if he insisted,

---

6   Fishing Creek, Kentucky, January 19, 1862.

7   Felix Kirk Zollicoffer of Tennessee was killed at Mill's Springs. Being very nearsighted and leading the advance, he was killed by a volley of Union fire.

8   Chickamauga, Tennessee, September 9-10, 1863.

9   Pleasant Hill, Louisiana, April 9, 1864.

he would make the charge himself, but would not order his men. He then turned to his men and told them of his being ordered to charge that battery, and was going to do so, but would not order them to do it. All the men in the regiment threw up their hats and told him that wherever he went they would go also. So he formed us into columns of fours, and we raised the "Texas Yell" and started on that fatal charge in which we lost our beloved Colonel. The Yankees hearing our yell, knew that we were coming. I supposed they had heard it before, for they limbered up their battery and carried it to the rear. We had hardly started before there was a courier sent after us with orders for us to turn to the left and get out of this death trap. However, it was too late to reach Col. Buchel, who was in front; but Col. Yeager took most of the regiment to the left and saved the greater part of the men.

M. D. Oliver of San Saba was not about to let a little thing like a head wound keep him from the war:

Was wounded on the head by a sharpshooter and was practically unconscious for three days, but as soon as I became rational I mounted my horse and reported for duty.

It was not healthy to be a flag bearer or even be close to one during battle, but **John A. Mathews of Swan** tells of an officer who pushed his luck even further:

Our first fight was at Shiloh,[10] *early in the morning of April 6, 1862. About sunrise we charged the Yankee encampment. Some were cooking and some were eating breakfast, and others were not up. We passed through their camps and a short distance beyond formed a line of battle. Our Colonel, T. Holzclaw, took our flag and rode up and down the line waving the flag and trying to make the enemy open fire on*

---

10   Shiloh, Tennessee, April 6-7, 1862.

us, but they would not do it. He then ordered up a piece of artillery and opened fire on them. It was like stirring up a hornet's nest. They soon let us know where they were.

There is a thin line between bravery and foolishness, and **Robert McGuire of McCaulley** reported on a general who knew the difference and practiced the better part of valor:

After some detouring we unexpectedly engaged the enemy at Perryville[11] on the evening of Oct. 8, 1862. Firing continued till after nightfall. We camped on the battlefield, having captured a good many guns. Next morning as Gen. Polk[12] was making the rounds he ran into the enemy and they hailed him to know who he was when he told them if they did not quit shooting he would show them who he was, though he was getting away as fast as he could.

Another leader had the courage to volunteer his men at Fredericksburg,[13] according to **Luther Wellington Murray of San Saba:**

About nine o'clock Gen. R. E. Lee, who was sitting on his horse near us, remarked that if he had one good regiment who would cross the ridge he thought the day would be won. Our commander said that he had one that would go, and we went. We lost 117 men in going down the bluff, but the day was won.

E. H. F. McMullen of Lufkin also testified to the bravado of a leader, perhaps with mixed emotions:

---

11 Perryville (Chaplin Hills), Kentucky, October 8, 1862.

12 Major General Leonidas Polk.

13 Fredericksburg, Virginia, December 13, 1862.

I will relate one little incident. At the Yellow Bayou[14] fight, Gen. Hardeman,[15] better known as "Gotch," when we were dismounted, for the fight, and were ordered to move slowly forward, some one raised the "Rebel Yell." Gen Hardeman was riding in front with drawn sword, yelled out, "I will lead you." Gen. Green,[16] when in command, always charged.

J. A. Moore of Clarksville quotes from the *Confederate Veteran* of June 1902 to support his report of an incident at the battle of Chickasaw Bayou:[17]

Does any old comrade who was in the battle of Chickasaw Bayou know the name of the bold rider who carried a dispatch from the extreme right of our line to the left? This was, indeed, a ride into the jaws of death. The courier had to ride parallel with the Federal lines for nearly two miles, and it is safe to say that not less than a thousand shots were fired at him, generally at close range. and as he came down the line, his hat held firmly in his teeth, his form erect, his long locks waving, dashing past us like a meteor, such a shout went up as possible was never heard before or since. Many daring feats were accomplished during the war, but none more so than this, and the hero at this time would have made a picture second to none for the easel of the most gifted painter. The route taken was the only direct one, for had he gone back of the bluffs, it would have made the distance some four or five miles out of the way, thus causing a delay which had to be avoided. It was said at the time that this daring rider was

---

14   Yellow Bayou (Bayou De Glaize, Norwood's Plantation, Old Oaks), Louisiana, May 18, 1864.

15   William Polk Hardeman.

16   Thomas Green, known for being impetuous.

17   Chickasaw Bayou, Mississippi, December 29-31 and January 1.

a Texan, and that he volunteered from the ranks to deliver the message, as no courier could be found, who was willing to undertake this hazardous task, the rider saying—"If you will furnish me a horse I will outrun the Federal bullets."

The answer came in the August issue of the *Confederate Veteran*, written by **W. T. Moore, Commander of Throckmorton Camp, U.C.V., McKinney, Texas**:

That soldier (my brother) is still living. Although it was a great miracle, he was allowed to get through that ride safely. He is the Rev. James A. Moore of Clarksville, Tex.

Ordinary men did extraordinary things when necessary, as reported by **Lewis M. Sheppard of Leggett**:

While in the ditches at Petersburg[18] I saw one of my commanders pick up a shell while it was smoking and throw it over the breastworks, and it struck the outside and exploded. This was a brave and daring act. I was next to him and by his quick action he saved several lives as well as his own. His name was J. A. Holland. He went through the war without a scratch, but the poor fellow died the same year the war closed of brain fever.

Dr. Frank Rainey of Dallas was a surgeon who found himself spending time on the firing line as well as in the field hospitals. He reported an unusual act of bravado from an unexpected source:

On this retreat when we got to Washington, just above Opalousas, La., we were making a stand as we did nearly every day, and just as we were hard pressed, a well-dressed matronly looking lady rushed in front of our troops and with frantic gestures, called to the soldiers to "Come on and let us

---

18 Campaigns took place at Petersburg, Virginia, in August and
October of 1864.

*whip the darned Yankees." This appeal so stirred up the Con-
federates that they charged with a tremendous yell, she being
in the lead, that for a time they completely routed a much
superior force. This was no doubt a good woman, but she had
been watching the progress of the fight 'til she could no longer
control herself, and this was in the way of an explosion.*

R. S. Philpott of Farmersville gave an account of another
bold woman:

*Was generally detailed as a scout, owing to the fact that I
had a good horse, but one day Will Holloway wanted some
books to read, and I went after them and rode his race mare.
The place was owned by a man named Tucker, and he had
some fine daughters, and I was sitting on the porch talking
to the young ladies, when the Yankees came upon me, and, as
I was not receiving company, went upstairs. The girl said,
"Give me your gun and they will not get your horse. You can
whip a dozen Yankees from upstairs." She stood them off.
They threatened to burn the house, but she said, "Burn it; it
will not be the first time." They did not get me nor my horse.*

J. H. Smith of Paris gave this account of yet another brave
lady:

*There was a cannon factory at Rome, Ga., and the Feder-
als were anxious to destroy it, and they had promised a
reward of $200.00 to each private and $500.00 to each officer
and a discharge from the army for its destruction. Col.
Streight, a brave though not very tactful officer, undertook
the job. He selected a fine looking lot of young men for the
work, and Gen. Forrest determined to defeat his plans, and it
became a race and a fight all the way. So closely did Forrest
pursue him that he had barely time to cross Black Creek and
burn the bridge. Miss Sansom told Gen. Forrest that she*

could show him a ford where he could cross and, mounting behind the General, with the bullets flying thick around her, rode up the creek a short ways and showed him the ford. The girl was about 14 years old and dressed in a homespun dress, which was made low in the neck and came just a little below the knees, and she was barefooted. Many were the young men who tipped their caps to the young lady and told her that when the war would be over they were coming to court her. A monument was erected to her memory at Gadsden, Ala., in recognition of her bravery. The thing which seemed to annoy the men under Col. Streight was that they surrendered to such an inferior force.

As the war wound down, the Confederates were desperate for men to bear arms, and **Aron Wilburn of Honey Grove** found that bravery does not have an age limit:

After the fighting around Atlanta, I became sick, and was again sent to the hospital and when I was able for duty, French's Division had fallen back to Mobile, Ala., and my last fighting was around Fort Blakely.[19] *At Mobile they called out every available boy over fourteen years and would put six of these boys with an old soldier on picket duty. Once it fell to my lot to take six of them out for duty and they all did good service. One noble fellow stood by me and shot at every opportunity. I told the boys if we were charged, for them to break for the breastworks as quick as possible. "I will not leave the rifle pit till you do." About 3 o'clock they came on us with three lines of battle and I told the boys to run. I took a shot and loaded my gun as soon as possible and looked up and they were real close and one man began to call, "Halt." But with shells and bullets flying thick I struck out*

---

19 Fort Blakely, Alabama, was under siege during March and April of 1865.

for the breastworks and when I had run about forty yards I jumped over the little boy with the top of his head shot off. I have no doubt that his parents never heard from him again or ever saw his corpse. I had to command this boy the second time to go to the breastworks.

A touch of kindness in the midst of battle was the memory **A. C. Swinburn of Vernon** had of the battle of Mansfield:

My Captain was killed at Mansfield,[20] and dark came on us in the hole and I got lost from my command, and in hunting my way out I found a Union soldier and he wanted me to carry him out, and I told him that I would not do it, but would leave him my canteen of water and some bread and meat, and left him and found my company at 12 o'clock that night, and was telling some of my company what I had found. I did not believe he would ever be found, as the country was rough and full of bushes. Next morning we followed up our victory, fought the battle of Pleasant Hill and gained a second victory. We followed the enemy and were gone some two weeks. When we returned we heard of someone being found that had lain on the battlefield for ten days and his chances of recovery were good, and that was the last we ever heard of him. Several years ago there was a man advertised in the Dallas News trying to find the man who gave him the bread and water at the battle of Mansfield, but I did not get his address, and would like to know it now, so that I might correspond with him.

Also at Mansfield, **George A. Watford of Merkel** relates his experience with a comrade in need:

---

20 Mansfield (Pleasant Grove, Sabine Cross Roads), Louisiana, April 8, 1864.

Very soon we received an order from Gen. Dick Taylor to come in great haste to Mansfield, La., and when we reached there he was sitting on his horse at a street corner and remarked as we passed; "Boys, I am glad to see you." We were sent as pickets in front of the enemy, and when we got in sight of them we were ordered to tie our horses in the brush and advance as infantry. My position on the left was in the timber, but the infantry was through the field. The crossing of that field was awful. The bullets were flying like hail and the shells were bursting, yet the infantry were marching bravely right into the jaws of certain death. As we approached the eastern side of the field our instructions were to keep going till the enemy was found, and when they proved too strong for us to fall back to the main line. We at last reached a fence; I stepped over it and took refuge behind a small post oak tree and about the size of a stovepipe. The Yanks spied me and commenced to shoot at me, and the bullets came pretty thick. One ball struck the tree and glanced onto my knee. This did not hurt, and it was the only ball that hit me during the war. I heard someone call, and looking around saw it was my nearest left-hand skirmisher; as he started to me he was shot down. His name was John Cranfield and he said: "For God's sake, Major, don't leave me here." I tried to lift him up, but found that I was not able. I could not resist his appeal, so I lay face down beside him and told him to take me around the neck and pull himself on my back, which he did, and I rose with him and carried him from under fire.

Capt. A. B. Barnes of Greenville gave an account of a heroic charge that saved the day for the Confederates:

In order that even the old soldier may understand our position I will try to describe it. Shelby's[21] Brigade, perhaps

1,100 strong, was the rear guard for Gen. Price's Army, consisting of about 8,000 men, many of them recruits and very poorly equipped. The brigade faced north with two ten-pound Parrott guns on our right, commanded by a one-armed Irishman named Kelly. On the north and north-west the whole face of the earth was blue with Federal Calvary, while on the northeast, distant about one-quarter of a mile, was a grove of black jack timber of six or eight hundred acres. Suddenly about 1,200 Federal Calvary, in columns of companies, appeared around that grove and coming directly towards our right flank. Hard pressed by at least 5,000 cavalry in front, our left threatened, and this new command, larger than our entire brigade, already on our right, certainly made it look like a show-down. Just then Gen Price[22] sent Gen. Shelby the following dispatch: "Remove your command one-half or three-fourths of a mile immediately south of your present position and take up the most practical position and hold the enemy at check till further orders." Gen. Shelby said: "Capt Barnes, your company and Capt. Orchard's company will please check those fellows coming down the hill." The order was repeated to the company when Major Kelly of the battery said; "Wait a minute, Captain, and I will help you." Then turning to the battery, "Action right rear. Double shot with canister, fire." Simultaneously I gave the order to charge. The effect was terrific. The Federal cavalry evidently considered us already captured and were coming directly on our flank without firing a shot. The double shotted guns literally tore the front of their column to pieces and immediately behind the death-dealing shot came the no less deadly cavalrymen. Close at hand they

---

21   General Jo Shelby of Missouri.

22   General Sterling "Pap" Price of Missouri.

fired their carbines and dropping them on their slings, they used their deadly revolvers and often at a distance of not more than six or eight feet, for the squadron charged squarely into the enemy's ranks, utterly and completely routing them. When the little band of eighty-three men returned they drove forty-seven horses with their equipment before them. They lost three men who were never heard of and seven or eight wounded. I do not think there is a parallel in history where eighty-six cavalrymen charged a column of 1,200, who believed themselves charging, utterly routing them.

When **Robert Agustus Brantley of Summerville** and the Fifth Texas overcame great odds at the Seven Days Battle[23] around Richmond, it earned them a word of praise from none other than Stonewall Jackson:

We marched on paths and through woods, slowly, all day, halting now and then, until we came to where Gen. Lee stood, and there we right faced for battle. When the order came to move forward, the Fifth Texas moved almost straight in front, meeting great bodies of straggling men with wounded coming out of the fight, sometimes breaking our ranks so bad that it kept up a confusion; they would implore us not to go, as it was certain death, the place was impregnable; we moved steadily on through brush and field until we were within 100 yards of Pow White Creek, just to the left of where the Fourth Texas crossed. We were then halted and ordered to file to the left upon the top of the hill fronting that terrible place at the head of Pow White Creek, which the stragglers said we could not take. There is no wonder that Gen. Jackson said: "These men that carried that place were soldiers indeed."

---

23   Seven Days Campaign, Virginia, June 25 to July 1, 1862.

William F. Glaze of Athens expressed some of the bravado of the men and the willingness to follow their leaders, regardless of cost:

When we arrived in Mississippi we were commanded by Gen Joseph E. Johnston. We got to Jackson, Miss., about dark one evening; it was raining a little, and we marched a short distance from the depot to camp. Next morning we were aroused by the drums beating the long roll, and we knew that it meant battle. We were soon in line, marching out on the Raymond road. We arrived at a farmhouse, formed in line of battle and waited perhaps an hour or more, and I began to think there was no enemy about; but I was mistaken. Our battery of six guns was placed in position in the yard on the right of our regiment, and in front of us was a gin house. There were some bales of cotton under the gin. As soon as our battery was in position they sent a shell over into the enemy's lines, where it exploded. It was answered by one which exploded just over our company, hurting no one; but the pieces of shell flew in every direction. A man in our company, W. T. Stillman, yelled out, "Look out, over there, Mr. Yank: you'll hurt someone if you don't mind." Soon the pickets were firing all along the line, and we knew the battle was on in earnest. We moved up to the gin, pulled those cotton bales out and strung them along for breastworks. Just then our Colonel stepped out in front and ordered us not to fire a gun till commanded. T. C. Morgan, then our Captain said: "Stand your ground, men, if there should come ten thousand." We cheered and said we would.

Frank Herron of Graham gave another account of how an officer could inspire the men to perform, even in the face of certain death:

After taking our place in line we could see our skirmishers falling back. This proved to me that we would soon be in a hot engagement. Never will I forget the picture of sadness on the faces of my comrades, the majority of whom were as still as death. Minutes seemed hours but we were not long in this suspense for as the Federal skirmishers came in sight our grand old Commander, Col. Walker, stepped out in front and calling "Attention," said; "We will soon be engaged in a battle and before we begin I wish to say that I do not command you to go, but to follow this old bald head of mine," and lifting his cap, gave the command, "Forward, Guide Center, March." In the twinkling of an eye sadness and despair vanished and in its place appeared a determination to conquer or die. Onward we went with the rebel yell, driving the enemy back through a corn field and across a deep narrow creek.

Southern bravery was obvious, but perhaps **William T. Gray of Fort Worth** may have exaggerated just a little in reporting a Yankee conversation:

Gen. Grant asked Gen. McClellan[24] why he fell back, and Gen. McClellan said: "The North Carolinians would charge with nothing but a Barlow knife."

---

24 Federal general George Brinton McClellan.

Index by Cities and Contributors

Other books from Republic of Texas Press